A BOY NAMED
COURAGE

A BOY NAMED
COURAGE

A SURGEON'S MEMOIR OF APARTHEID

Himmet Dajee, MD
with
Patrice Apodaca

CYNREN

PUBLISHED BY CYNREN PRESS
101 Lindenwood Drive, Suite 225
Malvern, PA 19355 USA
http://www.cynren.com/

Printed in the United States of America on acid-free paper

ISBN-13: 978-1-947976-00-9 (hbk)
ISBN-13: 978-1-947976-01-6 (pbk)
ISBN-13: 978-1-947976-02-3 (ebk)

Library of Congress Control Number: 2017963485

The authors have re-created events, locales, and conversations from their memories of them. To maintain their anonymity, in some instances, names of individuals and places have been changed.

Cover design by Emma Hall

For Bhanu,
who taught me how to dream

Contents

Prologue

MY HOME IN CALIFORNIA has a spacious balcony from which I can see, on a clear day, the shimmering Pacific Ocean in the distance, San Clemente and Santa Catalina islands nestled offshore, and miles and miles of spectacular coastline.

I bought this house many years ago, when I was at the pinnacle of my career as a surgeon. My oldest brother, Amrit, scoffed at me. "Why do you want such a big house when you live alone?" he demanded to know. I paid him no mind. I just wanted it and believed that at last I had earned a touch of comfort and peace from the thousands of hearts I had repaired over the years.

I had instantly fallen in love with the spiral staircase and the columns—columns!—in the grand foyer. The house had practical selling points too. It was in an ideal location just a short freeway drive away from the hospital where I'd set up my practice, a critical feature for a cardiac surgeon who existed pretty much always on call. In fact, the neighborhood was so popular with doctors that it went by the somewhat dubious nickname "Pill Hill."

Most of all, though, I yearned to sit on that balcony in the rare moments of solitude and introspection that a surgeon's life affords. I wanted to sit there and just be.

And sometimes, while I am on my balcony gazing out toward the water, I am transported back to South Africa.

Coastal Southern California resembles my native city of Cape Town in many ways: the deliciously seductive climate, the gorgeous ocean views, the beaches lined with palm trees, and the backdrop of slate-colored mountains rimmed by desert to the north and east. Sometimes from my balcony perch, I can spot the ships lined up out at sea, bound for the ports of Los Angeles and Long Beach to the north, and I'm reminded of my youthful jaunts with my brothers and a few cousins or friends to Cape Town's harbor to see the ships docked there.

When I was fourteen years old, in 1956, a conflict raging thousands of miles away sent ripples to my corner of the world. In July of that year, Egyptian president Gamal Abdel Nasser seized and nationalized the Suez Canal, the main shipping route for oil tankers and merchant vessels from the Persian Gulf to Europe and America. In October, Israeli, British, and French forces pushed toward the canal. The Soviets threatened to drop nukes, and the United States issued stern warnings to all parties.

But to my adolescent mind, the Suez Crisis presented a fortuitous opportunity for adventure. Over several months, thousands of ships were diverted around the Cape of Good Hope, and many of them docked at the Port of Cape Town to refuel and pick up provisions. Locals would line up quayside to greet the visitors. My pals and I were allowed to climb the ramps and board the ships and were given tours by the sailors.

It occurs to me now that those visiting vessels offered me a rare—perhaps the only—glimpse of freedom in my young life. The sailors came from far-off lands and spoke many different languages, but even though we were strangers, they would welcome my friends and me aboard, smile at us, tell us stories, and give us coins from their home countries. They treated us not as vermin but just as they would any other rambunctious boys. It didn't seem to matter to them that we had dark skin, and that astonished me to no end.

I believe that was when I first started to plan my escape.

Cape Town is magnificent to look at, no doubt, but to me, it was like a beautiful woman with a heart of stone who crushed my spirit again and again. Those visiting ships gave me a peek into other worlds—worlds where I believed I could one day leave behind the pain and daily humiliation of being a nonwhite in apartheid South Africa.

From a very young age, all I wanted was to leave my troubled homeland. As the son of Indian immigrants, I was well aware that I wasn't suffering the worst of the brutality and degradation that the Afrikaner government meted out to anyone whose skin wasn't white—day in and day out, I witnessed the savagery unleashed on the native blacks—but what we did endure was bad enough. I knew too well the fear and injustice that were routine under apartheid, and I hated the regime with a passion that grew fiercer with each passing day.

I admit, though, that I had other reasons for wanting to leave. Not only did the apartheid policies of segregation and subjugation make me an outcast in my own country but so too did my own people in our tight-knit community: my rigid, tradition-bound father, who wanted all his children to live in lockstep with the suffocating strictures of the Indian culture, and our network of friends and relatives, who could sometimes be just as racist and exclusionary as the merciless Afrikaners.

I didn't belong in either cage—not in the tormented existence of a nonwhite living under apartheid nor in the role of an obedient Indian boy who quietly accepts his lot. I never fit in, never felt as if I could truly breathe.

I came from two worlds, and I despised them both. Only by leaving could I prove my worth and learn truly and without hesitation what I was made of. My three older brothers, each in his own way, were forging their own paths. I would learn from them and draw strength from their examples. And then I, too, would make my own way.

As I grew, that became my deepest desire, my sole focus, my cause, my reason for being. I would leave South Africa one day, and I vowed that when I did, I would never look back.

If only it had been that simple.

Nothing was ever painless in South Africa—a fact that had been drilled into me for as long as I could remember—but there was no way I could have known just how difficult the road ahead would prove to be, just how easily I could have lost the battles I felt compelled to wage, how easily I could have succumbed to grief or despair, even after I had put an ocean between myself and the rot of my native country. I like to think that it was my steely determination alone that kept me forever pushing forward, that allowed me to devote my life to saving others. But I must admit that underneath my carefully cultivated, cool exterior, I harbored a reservoir of burning rage that has fueled my journey.

I was almost shamefully ambitious. I was relentless. But above all, I was angry.

It is only now, after a long life filled with love and loss, great success and utter failure, and a consuming desire to outrun my past, that I am at last coming to understand my own heart.

one

A BOY
NAMED COURAGE

I WASN'T EXPECTED TO SURVIVE.

Born two months premature, so tiny I could fit in the palms of my father's hands, I was nestled into a shoe box lined with cotton while my parents kept vigil, occasionally dipping their fingers in brandy and letting me suck the warm liquid from them. That I lived and eventually started to grow apparently came as a bit of a shock, and my mother always said it was because of the brandy. The other Indian ladies who came to visit when I was young would cluck and coo whenever they saw me, each time reminding me about the cotton-filled shoe box and how little and fragile I had been. "Eat," they always urged me, for I was such a scrawny kid that they were probably still half-convinced that I'd wither and collapse at any moment.

By the time of my early arrival in Cape Town, South Africa, on May 22, 1942, my parents already had three other sons. Amrit, named after a mythological Indian nectar that bestows immortality, was eight years my senior and the only one who had been born in India. Next was Bhanudey, known simply as Bhanu, a Hindi word for "sun," who was more than three years

1

older than me. After that came Dhiraj—his name means "calm" or "patience"—who was born a little more than a year before me.

I have no idea why my parents decided to name me Himmet. Perhaps it was a hopeful gesture, given that they weren't sure I'd live beyond my first month. Even when I did begin to thrive, I was plagued throughout my youth with the curse of low expectations. I don't know if my family and our friends in the Indian community thought I was slow-witted, exactly, but they certainly didn't think I'd ever amount to much, a point that was made abundantly clear to me on a daily basis. I was the runt of the family, the unremarkable kid who was so skinny and insubstantial that others took to taunting me with the insulting nickname "Slangetjie," which in Afrikaans means "snake."

I tried to ignore such slights, and in my darkest moments, I would remind myself that my real name carried far more significance and, I hoped, was a harbinger of the future I began to envision for myself. *Himmet,* in my parents' native Gujarati language, means "courage."

I was a lowly Indian boy, the fourth and largely discounted son of an immigrant family, and a nonwhite living among a ruling class that considered my kind worse than the dirt beneath its shoes.

But I was the boy named Courage, and I never forgot it.

My parents were probably no older than five or six when they became engaged.

My father, Govind Dajee, was born in 1913 to a low-caste family of cobblers in the tiny village of Tejlav in the Surat district of Gujarat, a rural state in western India that was also the birthplace of the great leader Mohandas "Mahatma" Gandhi. Our people weren't the lowest of the low, but their work with the finished hides of cows, which are considered sacred among Hindus, put my ancestors fairly near the bottom of the strict social hierarchy in India. My dad, like his father, and his father before him, had traveled to and from South Africa, part

Himmet's parents, Govind and Eicha "Kanta" Dajee.

of the diaspora of native Indians, who were then under British control, that reached to the far ends of the Empire in search of economic betterment. My mother, Eicha Dajee—Kanta to her family and friends—was born in 1915 and was promised to my father in the traditional way when they were both young children. Neither of my parents ever received a formal education. When he was thirteen, my father was sent off to South Africa to work in the family's shoe repair shop in Cape Town, returning to India seven years later to wed. My brother Amrit was born in Tejlav in 1934, after which my father moved his small family back to Cape Town to run the shoe business there.

There was nothing unusual about their story. Indians had been in South Africa since the earliest days of European settlement in the seventeenth and eighteenth centuries, when European colonists and traders brought them there first as slaves and later as indentured servants. After those practices ended, the steady stream of Indians emigrating from the mother country to South Africa continued. Indeed, Gandhi began his activism in South Africa in the early twentieth century as an immigrant lawyer who led a campaign of civil disobedience against laws that discriminated against Indians.

Despite its discriminatory policies, South Africa was still a place where low-caste, uneducated Indians like my parents could make a decent living as small merchants. The little Indian community in and around Cape Town in which I was raised was made up of a few hundred families just like our own—modest shoe merchants with roots in Gujarat, members of the lowly Mochi caste who stuck together and clung to the old, traditional ways even as the world around them underwent cataclysmic change.

When I was born in Cape Town in 1942, the world was at war, and the conflict could be felt even in a place as remote as the southern tip of the African continent. South Africa, a British territory for two hundred years, was officially on the side of the Allies and even sent some troops to fight against the Germans. But the country was deeply divided, for the Afrikaners, the descendants of Dutch and German settlers, loathed the British and sympathized with the Nazis. During the war, my father and all our friends and relatives lived in constant fear that German aircraft would swoop in and bomb the city. At night, they would close their curtains and dim their lights to reduce their chances of being targeted. Rumors circulated of German submarines off the coast of nearby Namibia, which was friendly to the Axis powers.

In 1947, two years after World War II ended, the Indian Independence Bill was passed, ending Britain's long reign and carving out the separate, independent nations of India and Pakistan. My father decided that it was time for us to make the trek back to India for a two-year stay. It was common practice among our friends and relatives to return to India to visit family members who were still there and to stay for many months, even years, as the trip was long and arduous. My dad left his shop in the care of friends and took his growing family—my sister Padma had been born in 1945—on a journey. We slept on the deck of a ship with other Indian families as we traveled up the east coast of Africa and across the Indian Ocean to Bombay.

Seated left to right, Amrit, Bhanu, Dhiraj, Himmet, and Padma, on board a ship bound from South Africa to India.

There we stayed for a short time in a relative's apartment, from which we could look out a window to the crowded, filthy street teeming with rats the size of small rabbits.

From Bombay, we traveled by train to Surat and then on to Tejlav. I have no clear memories of the trip, just the vague impressions and mental snapshots on which a young child tends to focus: ducks swimming in the river, the smoky aroma of dried salted fish, vendors selling tea and jackfruit. Our little village had no paved roads. We stayed in a modest, one-story house where my father's parents and two sisters lived, bookended by the houses of two uncles. Nearby were corn and rice fields, sugarcane plantations, and a mango orchard where we'd use long poles with hooks to pick the fruit. We took water from a communal well, where my brother Dhiraj got smacked once for touching the water jugs before the higher-caste people had filled theirs.

Certain scents and images have stayed with me over the years—the distinctive minty fragrance of eucalyptus trees, the brilliant blue and purple jacaranda blooms, and the sight of women hunched over open fires as they prepared our meals. When the monsoon rains came, it was quite the event. It wasn't cold, so we children would run outside and revel in the mud, paying no mind to the swarms of stinging red ants. We were warned to stay away from snakes, some of which were poisonous, and we were properly terrified, so much so that when a cricket ball got stuck in a tree, no one had the guts to climb up to retrieve it for fear of being bitten.

During the colorful Holi holiday, we painted our faces, dressed in costumes, and danced, and all the stomping feet destroyed our porch made of dung and clay. But there was plenty of clay to be found for repairs. Amrit would collect the reddish stuff from around a nearby dam and use it to sculpt little cow and buffalo figures.

My father, despite his traditional ways, was considered a bit of a progressive in our backwater. He would brag about his physical prowess and challenge the other men to wrestling matches and swimming races in the river, which he always won. When he bought a horse and carriage, it was the talk of the village, and he also purchased a used car so he could travel around the country. Though he had no formal education himself, he insisted that we all attend school, and he bought a radio so he and all the other villagers could gather around and listen to music and the news of the day.

He revered Gandhi. He talked about him constantly, quoting him, lecturing on and on about Gandhi's philosophy of passive resistance, telling us that he was a symbol of nonviolence and change in India and South Africa and, indeed, all the world. When we grew up, he told us, we must strive to live as Gandhi did and always be compassionate and understanding.

We were in Tejlav in January 1948 when the news came of Gandhi's assassination. People from the village gathered in front of our house to hear the reports on my father's radio. I remember the shock and anger, and the disbelief that it had been a Hindu man who had killed the Mahatma, the "great-souled one" of our people. A few weeks later, my father, distraught with grief, took my mother and Amrit to Delhi to

Himmet's father at a river in Gujarat. A fitness enthusiast, he was always challenging the other men to swimming races.

visit Gandhi's cremation site to pay their respects. My other siblings and I were told we were too young to go with them, so we stayed behind with relatives, understanding little of the forces that were shaping the world in which we lived.

During our long stay in India, our family grew again with the birth of my youngest sister, Hansa, in 1948. The following year, we embarked on the long voyage back to South Africa. Shortly after our return, we got the news that my grandfather had died back in India. The Cape Town business was now in the sole hands of my father.

two

THE AGE
OF APARTHEID

THE SOUTH AFRICA TO WHICH WE RETURNED had undergone momentous change in our absence. In 1948, the Afrikaner National Party had won control of the government. The age of apartheid was upon us.

My father always used to say to us that an Afrikaner will tell you to your face that you are worthless shit. The British, on the other hand, will smile and speak to you in a civil manner, but when your back is turned, they'll stick a knife in it. The message was clear: all whites hated our guts, and we mustn't ever forget it. Even so, my father and his contemporaries must have known that with the Afrikaners in power, we were heading from bad to worse.

White supremacy and racial segregation had been the de facto policy in South Africa long before apartheid, but the Afrikaners took those policies to new, ruthless extremes, justifying their actions by claiming their biblically ordained superiority. *Apartheid* in the Afrikaans language means "separateness," a simple philosophy that was carried out with a comprehensive brutality. We Indians were classified separately from the blacks and from the coloreds—people of mixed race—but all

9

of the nonwhites were regarded in virtually every way with utter contempt.

The government began passing a series of laws intended to keep the whites on top and everyone else crushed under its heel. The Afrikaners took land away from nonwhites, often forcibly removing people from their homes, tossing their belongings into the street, and confining them to tightly congested ghettos where resources were scarce and poverty and desperation prevailed. They limited the places where nonwhites were allowed to go—just traveling from one province to another required a special governmental pass. Strict curfews were violently enforced, and sexual relations and marriage between whites and nonwhites were banned. The Afrikaners were brutish, but they were also cunning. They used their apartheid laws, and the enforcement of those laws, to pit different races and native tribes against each other to tighten their own grip on power. Chinese South Africans, for instance, were treated similarly to Indians, but those of Japanese ancestry were given "honorary white" status, meaning they had more rights than we did, although, like us, they were not allowed to vote.

Like the racist policies of the Jim Crow South in the United States, apartheid forced separation among the races in almost every aspect of life: in schools; on buses; in restaurants, stores, and parks; and in governmental offices and workplaces. Nonwhites were banned from owning certain businesses and holding certain jobs, and even if they had the same job as a white, they'd be paid far less. Signs were everywhere: "Whites Only" for the best places and "Nonwhites" for the leftovers. Cape Town is renowned throughout the world for its beautiful beaches with sand that glistens like sugar, but in those days, the "Whites Only" signs stood in warning that such places were off-limits to my kind. The only beaches we were allowed to visit were those with jagged rocks instead of soft sand. At the drive-in cinema, we were only allowed to park our cars in the back row. Daring to go where we weren't allowed carried the risk of imprisonment. If a whites-only ambulance on an emergency call arrived to find that the person in need of help had dark skin, the driver would turn the vehicle around and leave.

As the apartheid government began its long campaign of racial suppression, my family nonetheless slipped quickly back into our life in South Africa. My father's shop was on Sir Lowry Road, a main thoroughfare running through the center of Cape Town. Our store was one in a long row of small businesses. On one side of us was a confectionary shop owned by a Jewish couple, who we could see through their window as they slept upright in the reclining chairs they used instead of beds. We interpreted their unusual sleeping arrangement as a sign of the frugality that was common among the local merchants and to a lack of usable space in their tiny store. On the other side of us was a Muslim butcher, at whom we used to laugh as he waved his meat cleaver and chased his workers around the shop and out into the street when they didn't follow his orders.

When the forced removals began across South Africa under the Group Areas Act of 1950, our neighborhood was exempted—at least for the time being—so my family and our neighbors were allowed to stay and continue to serve clientele of all races. We were surrounded by big factories, where everything from pharmaceuticals to ladies' clothing was made. Once, the Baumanns Biscuit factory a couple of blocks away caught fire, and the whole neighborhood smelled like baking cookies. The company had to unload its inventory, so we stocked up on so many tins of biscuits at a fraction of the usual price that we were still eating them a year later.

My father's shop had two big display windows in front where his newfangled neon sign flashed in bright red the words "Shoe Repair." Just inside was a small counter where we kept the cash register, and on the other side of the shop were the Landis machines that were used to cut the big sheets of leather that we bought from a wholesaler on Buitekant Street. After the forms were cut, we used other machines to sand, glue, nail, and sew the shoes. The whole place reeked of shoe glue mixed with the earthy smell of treated cowhides, and though we had

Himmet's father in front of his shoe store on Sir Lowry Road
in Cape Town.

a big vacuum to suck up the leather dust, fine layers of it settled everywhere, coating the shelves, sticking to the floor that my siblings and I swept each day, and probably adding to the suffering of my asthmatic mother.

A door at the back of the shop led to the few rooms that we called home. There was a small parlor, which doubled as a dining room and a bedroom for my brothers and me. Next to that was a kitchen, and behind the parlor was a bedroom that my parents shared with my two little sisters. Off a small alleyway just out back was a toilet, a shower with water heated from a wood furnace, and a pigeon coop. Our roof was made of corrugated zinc. When it rained, it sounded as if the gods were pelting us with pebbles from on high, and when the southeastern winds swept across the Cape each spring, the constant rattling above our heads would jangle our nerves.

It was a modest lifestyle, to be sure, but we were comfortable and well fed. My dad was a clever businessman, always looking for ways to expand and improve. He would tell us about his hard life in the early days when he would ride his bicycle all over the city, carrying sacks of shoes and making pickups and deliveries at the back doors of white people's houses, because they wouldn't allow him to approach by the front. He always had new ideas, though, and he soon began selling shoes as well as repairing them. Later he bought up a huge supply of old army uniforms left over from the war, which he resold in the shop at a big markup. Soon he added other clothing, and my brothers and I would laugh as we dressed the mannequins in the front windows and adjusted their arms and legs into strange poses. When he added ladies' nylons to the inventory, they flew off the shelves. He made enough of a profit that he began investing in other businesses, such as a dairy distribution firm, and in real estate, buying a few buildings on his own or in partnership with friends in areas where Indians were allowed to hold property.

A proud, upright man, my dad had firm opinions. In my mind, I can still replay some of his lectures on the importance of education, exercise, hard work, and tradition. We children weren't his only audience. He held various leadership positions in the Cape Town chapter of a countrywide organization for Indians of our caste. The group was called Kshatriya Mochi Mitra Mandel. Kshatriya was the name for the warrior caste, Mochi was our caste, *mitra* means "friends," and *mandel* is another word for "temple." My father would give speeches at our local chapter's regular meetings in which he invariably addressed some version of "Keeping Our Indian Identity Intact." He stayed on his soapbox at home, where he would lecture to us that Indian culture had endured for thousands of years, which proved that it was superior to all other cultures. Then he would grow angry with me when I challenged him on his beliefs, pointing out to him that many Indians lived amid poverty, filth, and corruption. He would shout at me in

Gujarati, reprimanding me for my lack of appreciation and respect for my Indian heritage. He was right, I was wrong, end of discussion.

When I was young, I saw my father as a passionate and persuasive patriarch, larger than life one moment but a mass of contradictions the next. He was fastidiously thrifty most of the time, always reminding us to use only as much as we needed, whether it was food, clothes, or gasoline, and negotiating prices on everything, even items as small as a piece of fruit. But when it came to certain treasured possessions, only the best would do, like his top-of-the-line Grundig reel-to-reel tape recorder, on which he would play the clanging Indian music that jarred my ears, and his beloved Rover, colloquially known as the poor man's Rolls-Royce, which he would use to take us on drives to the mountains and beaches.

My dad was also a fitness nut. He loved doing headstands and would constantly praise the virtues of yoga, Ayurvedic medicine, and healthy eating. He liked to think of himself as a well-respected authority figure in our community—which I suppose he was, to some extent—and he made it clear that he expected his sons to assume similar positions one day.

Many nights, he would sit at our kitchen table with his friends and play cards; sip brandy or whiskey; smoke cigars, cigarettes, or a pipe; and hold forth on all the political topics of the day that he'd heard about on the radio or read of in the many publications he collected—everything from *Life* magazine to the Gandhi-founded newspaper the *Indian Opinion*. He spoke incessantly about the Phoenix Settlement, a communal farm that Gandhi had started and that had become a center of activism and resistance.

One night, as his friends gathered in our kitchen, one of them, noticing my skin-and-bones frame, quipped that I looked like the slain civil rights icon, in reference, I suppose, to Gandhi's famous hunger strike. The nickname stuck, and for years—decades even—my brothers would occasionally refer to me as "Gandhi." Much better than "Slangetjie," I reasoned.

There was no doubt what my enterprising father had in mind for his family. He wanted his sons to take over the business one

Himmet's mother with his oldest brother, Amrit.

day and continue on in the same way that he lived: working the trade, maintaining the same close ties to our Gujarati community, marrying obedient Indian girls, and making sure that our younger sisters found suitable Indian husbands. It would never have occurred to him to ask if that was what we wanted. With my dad, it was always "the community this" and "the community that." He wanted his children to be smart and well educated, but then he erected walls around us by insisting that we confine ourselves only to "the community."

If my father was domineering, my mother was just the opposite. She was in many ways the quintessential Indian woman. Kind, quiet, and subservient, she spoke not a word of English and always wore traditional saris, covering her head as a show of respect when visitors called. The constant bouts of asthma that left her weak, wheezing, and gasping for breath much of the time only reinforced the appearance of complete submissiveness. I remember a doctor who treated her regularly, who would arrive in theatrical fashion on horseback, instructing her to breathe in and out as he listened to her chest with obvious concern.

But underneath my mother's meek veneer, I always detected a core of resolve and steadfast love for her children. When I think of her, I remember her gentle pat on my head, a protective, affectionate gesture that made me feel that she was on my side and would always look out for me. I loved her. It was just that simple, and I couldn't imagine life without her.

Our lives were dictated by routine. On weekdays, we would rise early and do our morning chores, taking turns making beds, assembling sandwiches for our lunches, and washing the breakfast dishes. My mother liked to fix breakfast for us, but she was often too exhausted, or even confined to a hospital bed for days on end, so many days, we children quietly prepared our own meals. Before we left, my father tuned in to a radio program devoted to fitness and ordered us to follow along with

Himmet, Bhanu, and Dhiraj, left to right, behind the family shoe store and living quarters in Cape Town.

the exercises, touching our toes, windmilling our arms, and jumping rope, before he'd let us leave the house.

We walked to school. For my first two years, I attended the Anglican-run Saint Phillips Primary School. Then I moved on to the government-run Zonnebloem Primary School. When I was seventeen, I entered the two-year Trafalgar High School, which was also a public school. All these schools were strictly nonwhite, and my classmates were Indian kids, coloreds, and Malays. We wore the standard-issue uniforms: gray shorts, blue blazer, white shirt, blue tie, and gray cap, with a brown leather satchel for our books worn crosswise over one shoulder. If not for our brown skin, we could have passed for buttoned-down British schoolchildren.

After school, we hurried home for a quick snack before boarding a bus to go to Indian school, where we studied math, Indian history, and the Gujarati language. We would return in the evening, and it was only after dinner and more chores that we were able to tackle our homework. My father deplored idleness, and he never allowed his children an unoccupied moment.

I was a singularly unremarkable student. I loved history, but even my grades in that subject were only fair to middling. Most of the time, I struggled and stumbled along, distinguishing myself in absolutely nothing. As I grew older, I began to realize, and resent, how all the coming and going, pushing and pulling in various directions, hindered my ability to concentrate and achieve better results. At school we were forced to learn the hated Afrikaans language as well as English. We needed to be fluent and pass exams in both of these languages if we were to have any hope of going to university. But then we switched to Gujarati for our Indian studies, and at home our father demanded that we speak only Gujarati. If we slipped into English, he'd reprimand us, and increasingly, my brothers and I fought back. My father expected us to be knowledgeable about other cultures and political systems, but he also wanted us to accept and endure our small, suffocating way of life. We couldn't understand how a man who insisted on all of us getting a modern education could remain so stuck in the past. As I grew up, it became harder and harder for me to reconcile all the contradictions.

I also found it difficult to study at home, where running the business always took precedence and we fought for space on our cramped kitchen table. And the older I grew, the more I felt the acute and pervading hopelessness of life as a nonwhite. I would try to work harder and study more, take my books to the library where there were fewer distractions and I could focus. But nothing helped. I couldn't shake the voices in my head telling me I was just a dumb good-for-nothing.

Of course, the voices weren't just in my head. I could see the dismissive looks on the faces of the Afrikaners and hear the contempt in their voices. Many whites called us by the racist label "coolie." I would seethe with shame and anger every time I walked down the street, only to find myself shrinking away from those whites who acted as if they—and only they—were entitled to every bit of the earth.

Once when I was in my early teens, my brother Dhiraj, some friends, and I decided to challenge the whites-only rule at a local movie theater. *Around the World in 80 Days* was playing, and we were determined to see it, so we dressed in our best clothes and strode up to the ticket office. I was trembling with fear and excitement, but to my surprise, they let us in, with the warning that we could sit only in the very back row and that if we made any noise, we'd be booted out. We didn't utter a peep and made it through to the end. Afterward, when we told our parents what we'd done, they called us crazy and had a hearty laugh.

Even as a child, I understood that not all whites were monsters. Although we weren't allowed to attend school with white students, some of our teachers were white, and many probably secretly despised apartheid and sympathized with us. One of the reasons I loved history, particularly by the time I got to high school, was that many of the history teachers— mainly the colored ones, but also a few whites—were socialists who weren't afraid to voice their hatred of apartheid and the Afrikaners. Indeed, Trafalgar High School was well known as a hotbed of liberalism. We students would sometimes march to the police barracks with our teachers to protest against segregation, and I would hear talk of clandestine meetings that some faculty members organized to plan anti-apartheid activities.

It was a dangerous line they toed, for if they had been caught speaking against the government or enlisting students in the protest movement, they would undoubtedly have been jailed, or worse. They warned us continually not to discuss politics in public, and so great was my fear that I even thought twice about my answer to an essay question on a final exam, which required me to write about the effects of increasing automation. I answered that one likely effect would be that more people would lose their jobs. The first thing that went through my mind after I turned in the test was that the government might peg me as a labor sympathizer.

One of my classmates at Trafalgar was Basil February, a young colored man who later became something of a folk hero for his militant activism against apartheid. Though he was two years younger than me, we were in the same class in high school, and I remember him well as a great guy, bright and

19

Trafalgar High School students, including Dhiraj, second from left, and Basil February, far right, who later became an anti-apartheid activist and folk hero.

charismatic, with a cropped-top haircut. When he was just twenty-three, he was gunned down in what was then Rhodesia, now Zimbabwe, after he attempted to cross the border back into South Africa. Authorities and eyewitnesses have given many conflicting accounts, but everyone I knew believed that South African police forces either ordered or carried out the killing.

Such violent outcomes were not uncommon. Every day in my youth, we heard news of people being arrested on what everyone knew were minor or trumped-up charges. We saw blacks in the street outside our shop caught by police for not carrying their government-required passbooks or for being outside of their designated areas past curfew. Sometimes it seemed as if they were arrested just for being black. The cops would beat them without mercy and toss them into the backs of the police wagons like sacks of potatoes. I often wondered if they were ever seen again.

Sometimes, especially on weekends, I saw black men out in the street, drunk and belligerent, and I understood that they were driven by despair. Fights broke out, and the police rounded everyone up, beating them with indiscriminate ferocity. The Afrikaners never asked questions out of concern. They were never interested in improving anyone's lot but their own. They herded the blacks like animals, calling them names like "kaffir," a slur with the same awful potency as "nigger." Every day I would watch how the native blacks were mistreated in their own country, and my heart bled for them.

Sometimes black and colored people came into our shop, and my father tried to engage them in conversation, asking about how apartheid had affected them. Young as I was, I was interested in their stories and paid close attention. I could tell that many were reluctant to speak, knowing that if they said the wrong thing to the wrong person, they could be arrested. But I recall one particularly candid colored guy telling my father that he had served in World War II as a driver in Italy. Because he wasn't white, he wasn't allowed to carry a gun, but the Italian people treated him decently. "Then I come back here and it's the same. I'm treated like shit again," he told my father.

We Indians weren't immune to mistreatment. The Afrikaners resented our business acumen and industriousness, and nonwhites widely acknowledged that the Afrikaners saw us as a threat to their claims of superiority. Laws were enacted to prevent Indians from becoming middle class and competing with the Afrikaners—laws, for example, that sharply restricted Indians' ability to buy businesses and property. It wasn't uncommon for Indians to join the African National Congress (ANC) and other anti-apartheid organizations. But many stayed quietly on the sidelines out of fear or because they figured that, since we Indians didn't have it quite as badly as the blacks, why take the risk? My father always cautioned us to trust no one; that spies were everywhere, even possibly among our friends; and that one wrong move could land us in jail. So that was how we lived—always on guard, never trusting anyone's motives, forever expecting the worst. Perhaps those perpetual feelings of fear and mistrust made us cling even more tightly to our traditions and the small comforts of our humble home.

three

ALWAYS AN
OUTSIDER

AS CHILDREN, WE KNEW WHAT WAS EXPECTED OF US, and at least at first we did as we were told. I remember draping our wet laundry on a line hung across the tiny space out back and then, in the winter, moving the line into the kitchen, where we'd have to maneuver around the damp clothes. We had no refrigerator, just a man who came round regularly with blocks of ice, but primitive as that might seem, it also meant that the food we ate was fresh. When the fishmonger's horn blew as he passed down the street, we knew our dinner that night would be seafood just plucked from the waters off the Cape.

Once a week, we'd visit a farmer's market a couple of miles away, and we'd load up on all manner of fresh produce—watermelon, papaya, bananas, cabbage, cilantro, carrots, and eggplants—that my mother and aunts would use to make all the traditional Indian dishes. Some of the meals were so spicy that they made me sneeze, but I was accustomed to them and didn't mind. We children had our parts to play; one of our jobs was to make the garam masala, a potent mixture of chili, pepper, and spices that we'd grind into a fine blend with a mortar and pestle.

I had a special duty. Sometimes we'd keep chickens in the backyard coop, and I was the designated executioner. I don't know why I got this job, and I'm sure today it would horrify some vegetarians I know, but I used to love doing it, probably because it meant that we would have a delicious, fresh chicken for dinner that night. I was ruthlessly unsentimental about it. I would grab a chicken and decapitate it with one swift hatchet chop, letting the blood ooze away in the drain below. I'd put it in hot water for a few minutes to make it easier to pluck, then my brothers and I would strip the feathers while it was still in the water. After that, I'd slice off the parson's nose—that's the tail end—and cut the bird into pieces. My mother would cook the chicken in a big pot with onions, tomatoes, and, of course, a medley of fragrant spices that would set my mouth watering. We'd eat the finished stew with lentils, rice, and a green salad dressed with white vinegar.

On Sunday, the only day when our shop was closed, Mom made puri, a fried pastry that puffed up in hot oil; a flatbread called roti; and thin crisps called papad. For the most special occasions, we ate curried crayfish, and that was a real treat. When I was a teenager, I'd sometimes go with a group of friends down to Cape Point, where we'd cast nets into the water with bait, hauling in as many as twenty or thirty crayfish, which we'd feast on later.

On the weekends, we boys also played cricket and tennis and climbed flat-topped Table Mountain, one of Cape Town's most famous landmarks. Occasionally, we'd join with other families on overnight trips to the camping grounds in the mountains at Steenbras Nature Reserve, where we would stay in a forested area in round, thatched-roof rondavels and the men would grill lamb kebobs on big outdoor fire pits.

Of course, Sundays were always reserved for prayer meetings. The Hindu temple we attended along with all the other members of our Gujarati community wasn't grand or ornate like some of the temples in India. Quite the opposite: it was an ordinary hall, which doubled as a meeting place for our table tennis club and was sometimes rented out for parties and other functions. But it did the job well enough.

I don't think my parents were particularly pious, but observing the Hindu faith was such an ingrained part of our culture that

Table Mountain, an iconic site in Cape Town. Its famous flat top
is often draped in clouds, like a tablecloth.

it never would have entered their minds to question it. Going
to temple was more of a social event, where we would meet up
with all our friends and relatives to catch up on the gossip and
goings-on.

I would sit through the prayer meetings, breathing in the
aroma of burning sandalwood, incense, and ghee, gazing
distractedly at pictures of deities like the eight-armed Shiva,
and listening to the chanting and singing, without really taking
any of it in. Much of it I wouldn't have fathomed even if I had
tried. The prayers, led by a priest in white robes, switched back
and forth from Gujarati to Hindi, which is related to Gujarati but
not so closely that I could follow along, and then to the Sanskrit
passages in the Hindu scripture known as the Gita, which I
didn't understand either. It was all as incomprehensible to me
as Middle English, or like trying to follow a Catholic Mass in
Latin. It was a big mishmash, and so I tuned out and waited for
the service to end so I could chat with my buddies. I never felt a
connection to the Hindu faith and only vaguely comprehended
all the deities and rituals and the idiosyncrasies of its philosophy
of reincarnation. As usual, I felt like an outsider.

At home the radio was always on, and we subscribed to two newspapers, the *Cape Times,* which arrived every morning, and *Cape Argus* in the evening, as well as *Life* magazine. My father was a news junkie, always interested in hearing about world events. We learned from my father about the Nuremberg trials, the United Nations, and the deliberations of the U.S. Congress. I remember in particular my dad's rants about John Foster Dulles, the U.S. secretary of state of the Eisenhower administration, who tacitly supported South Africa's apartheid policies because he saw the Afrikaner-led government as a bastion against communism.

I was mesmerized. I reveled in the discussions about politics and world events; and yet, here again, I felt a dichotomy.

Unlike my Gandhi-quoting father, I couldn't quite relate to the concept of passive resistance, which among the Indians I knew in South Africa seemed more like plain old passivity and acquiescence. And, all too often, I sensed the hypocrisy and narrow-mindedness prevalent among my people. I was Indian, yes, but I was also a South African, and I admired the passion and courage of Nelson Mandela and other anti-apartheid leaders far more than I ever identified with Gandhi. I even began keeping a scrapbook of news clippings about Mandela, which for many years was my most prized possession.

Perhaps this was what moved me to take a stand against my own kind when I was about fifteen years old.

I had invited a school friend, who happened to be colored, to join the table tennis club that met in the same hall where we held our religious services. It was called the Universal Table Tennis Club. Universal, my foot. Many members objected to including my friend, saying our club was for Indians only. So it was put to a vote, and my friend and I lost overwhelmingly. I was disgusted. Here were these guys spouting all this high-minded talk about the evils of apartheid and the need for racial harmony, yet they endorsed segregation themselves when someone just a little bit different got too close.

So I did the only thing I felt to be right at the time: I resigned from the club. I was outraged that the same people who felt the constant sting of discrimination were excluding my friend

Himmet, Dhiraj, and Bhanu, left to right, in the family parlor behind the shoe store. Their father insisted that they all read *Life* magazine and stay informed about world events.

because he wasn't one of us. Looking back, my protest might seem like an insignificant gesture, a spit into the wind, but at the time, it created quite a stir in our little community and added to the growing reputation of the Dajee boys. On one hand, we were often referred to as *vaghs,* or "tigers," a flattering way of depicting us as tenacious fighters. Often, however, we were just called disrespectful and rebellious.

In truth, we were different; I have no doubt about that.

Amrit, the eldest, was reserved by nature and the most traditional and dutiful of my father's sons, but even he stood apart from the other Indians we knew. He was brilliant—such an outstanding student that he was one of only a handful of nonwhites and only the second from our Indian community to be accepted into the medical school at the prestigious University of Cape Town, which made him a big deal among our friends and relations. We weren't really close when I was young, because he was so much older, but I admired him greatly and wished that I could be as smart and accomplished as he was.

Dhiraj, who was closest to me in age, had a quiet and easy-going manner, but then he did something shocking: he fell in love with a colored girl. When my father found out, he hit the roof and forbade Dhiraj from seeing her. Dhiraj refused to drop her, and that decision ultimately led to my father and our entire community shunning him. Once again, I was appalled by the narrow-mindedness of my father and his contemporaries, and I deeply respected my brother for standing up for himself and his convictions.

And then there was Bhanu. Although he was more than three years my elder, I was closer to him than to anyone else in the world. Bhanu was a handsome charmer and unabashed optimist whose kindness and charisma were infectious. He was the one and only person among all my family and peers who I felt really believed in me; indeed, many times, his encouragement alone kept me going when everyone else had written me off as a loser. I loved him so much that once, when I was in primary school, I cried and cried because he was absent from school that day and wasn't there to console me after I was reprimanded for having a dirty collar. I imagined him putting an arm around my shoulder, as he often did, and telling me, "Don't worry, Himmet, I'm here. I'll always be here for you." As we got older, our bond grew deeper still.

Yet, strangely, in some ways, Bhanu, with his entrepreneurial spirit and business instincts, was the one most like my father and the one among us who was probably best suited to take over the family business and leadership position in our community. Everyone liked him—it was impossible not to—and just like my dad, he would gather his friends around for drinks, card games, and conversation.

But Bhanu also wanted to go his own way and build something all his own. When he was only about seventeen, he decided not to go to high school, and he opened a shoe shop a couple of blocks from ours in one of the buildings that my father owned.

Bhanu preparing food in his Cape Town restaurant, Granita.

When his business failed, instead of giving up, he changed gears. He got a job as a waiter at the fancy La Perla restaurant in downtown Cape Town, and he made it a point to study the operation and ask lots of questions. Using the knowledge he picked up there, he opened his own restaurant in the same building as his failed shoe shop, while living in the rooms in the back. He called the establishment Granita, and he served an eclectic mix of food ranging from Indian curries and samosas to hot dogs and hamburgers, which attracted a steady clientele from the bus depot next door.

As I watched my older brothers break away and forge their own paths—Amrit, the brilliant, shooting star; Dhiraj, the shy rebel; and Bhanu, my best friend and protector—I began to obsess over my own future.

I was consumed with hatred for the Afrikaners. One day, when I was about fifteen, I was stopped by a policeman as I ran down the street on my way from my father's shop to Bhanu's place. "Why are you running?" he demanded to know, eyeing me as if I must be carrying stolen goods. He let me go when he saw that I had nothing, but it wasn't until I made it to Bhanu's that I realized how hard I was shaking, whether more from fear or anger I couldn't say. At the same time, I was also growing increasingly detached from the Indian culture in which I had been raised. I desperately wanted to run away from a world that I knew firsthand could be cold, hostile, and unforgiving, to leave all that bitterness and alienation behind. But I couldn't just run away—I needed something to run toward.

Then something happened that made my world colder still.

four
A COLDER WORLD

MY MOTHER WAS BACK IN THE HOSPITAL after a particularly bad asthma attack. I was worried, because the bouts of illness were becoming more frequent and increasingly severe, and she had been particularly frail and disheartened. She was so weak at times that Bhanu had to lead her by the hand to visit his restaurant just a few blocks away. Treatments back then were woefully inadequate—the anti-inflammatories and bronchodilators that are widely used today weren't yet available in our community in South Africa—and I could see that the struggle to breathe was taking a heavy toll. Sometimes Mom became so starved for air that she'd have to go to the hospital in the middle of the night; other times, we'd return from school to find her gone, and we knew what had happened. It had become almost routine, and yet I could tell from her drawn face, stooped posture, and growing fatigue that her condition was worsening.

As I awoke one morning in March 1958, about two months shy of my sixteenth birthday, in the sofa bed I shared with Dhiraj, I could hear my father talking softly into the phone that hung just on the other side of the wall, in an alcove inside our little shop. I had to listen closely, because his voice was so faint, but I could just make out out his words, and my heart sank.

My mother was dead.

I looked over at Dhiraj, who was also now awake.

"Did you hear that?" He nodded. We stared at each other and then started to cry. Soon Padma and Hansa were awake, and when they heard the news, they were inconsolable. Bhanu and Amrit arrived, and other relatives and friends began showing up, the women folding my little sisters into their arms, huddling in a trembling bundle as they tried to comfort the girls.

It all seems like a blur to me now. I remember my father taking over, being organized and methodical, calling the funeral home and planning the service. In the Hindu faith, funerals are typically held immediately, so everything happened very quickly.

The casket bearing my mother's body soon arrived, and people continued to show up, filling our little home to capacity. Prayers were chanted. Women began cooking, because after the service, the men and boys would come back—in those days, it was our custom that only males attended cremation ceremonies—and they would need to be served traditional vegetarian dishes along with the glasses of brandy, scotch, and other spirits that would be raised to toast my mother's memory and wish her spirit well on its journey.

When it was time to leave, the men in my family carried the casket to the hearse. My father and brothers and I rode behind the hearse in a black sedan. Silence punctuated the somber mood.

At the cemetery—the one we went to was for nonwhites, of course, because even in death, we had to be segregated—I saw my mother's shrouded body lifted from the casket and laid on top of an open pyre stacked high off the ground in an outdoor area used specifically for cremations. The fire was lit, and as the priest chanted, the flames rose and consumed the wood, along with my mother's remains. My father used to tell us that we needed to be as good as possible in this life so that we would rise to a higher level in the next life and ultimately reach nirvana. The funeral service is a part of that process; our spirits are released from this earthly realm by becoming wind and fire, and then they await reincarnation. We would later bring the ashes home in a copper urn to spread them in the ocean when we felt ready. I had been to many of these services before, and so I knew what to expect, and I understood that the spirits of the dead were believed to live on, to be rewarded later for their goodness.

But this time, it wasn't just some abstract concept; it was my mom. She had been the heart of our family, the buffer that had softened my father's sharp edges, the gentle and loving center of my world. I was supposed to believe that she had gone to a better place, but as the smoke rose into the sky and dissolved into wispy trails, I could only think that I would never see her again. Though I knew how sick she had been and how much she had suffered, I was still just a fifteen-year-old boy. Many years would pass before I learned that an autopsy had revealed that in addition to her respiratory illness, my mother had been suffering from pancreatic cancer. The proximate cause of death is something I'll never know, but as a young man, it didn't make any difference to me. She was gone, and that was all that mattered. As the sun grew dim, I watched in stunned silence as the flames died and what was once my mother was reduced to ashes. I kept asking myself, *What's going to happen to us now?*

It didn't take long to find out.

Immediately after my mother died, my father became aloof. He would often leave without explanation, and soon we learned why: he was already seeing another woman, a divorcée named Sharda. Within a year they were married, and our new stepmother, a virtual stranger, had moved into our home.

As Sharda took over running our household, my father grew even more distant, and the atmosphere at home became increasingly strained. My siblings and I had many questions we wanted to ask but dared not. Why did our father marry again so quickly? Didn't he realize how hard that might be for us, so soon after our mother's death? Why would our father, who cared so deeply about his standing in our community, risk becoming the center of gossip and speculation with his hasty marriage?

At first we stayed quiet, but the situation at home grew more and more tense. Unlike my gentle mother, we considered Sharda to be stern, remote, and always disapproving of our motives and actions. My siblings and I were still deeply grieving, yet we never heard a word of comfort, affection, or sympathy from our new stepmother. Instead, she rode my little sisters constantly about their chores and made it clear that she expected the girls to be married and gone by the time they turned eighteen. Dhiraj and I, the only boys still living at home, were older and more difficult to control, but Sharda was intent on exerting her new authority. When she told us we could no longer take clothes from the shop to use as our own, as we had always done, we felt insulted. My father, who had never minded before, sided with his new wife.

Bhanu came to our rescue. Dhiraj and I hadn't yet finished high school, but seeing how unhappy we were, Bhanu told us we were welcome to move in with him, and we eagerly agreed.

My father took our plan as a slap in the face and insisted we stay. "What will the community think?" he demanded. That was his go-to argument: we mustn't do anything to risk reproach in the community. But Bhanu stood his ground against my father. He told him that Dhiraj and I weren't happy and that it didn't matter what the community thought. He even made it clear to Padma and Hansa that as soon as they were old enough, they could have a home with him as well. In that moment, Bhanu became even more of a hero to me than ever.

So Dhiraj and I moved into the rooms behind Bhanu's restaurant. Dhiraj later began a pharmaceutical apprentice-ship and moved in with his girlfriend, Belle; they eventually married. Unhappy as my father had been with us for leaving home, he had grudgingly come to terms with it. But Dhiraj's marriage was a step too far. With a dramatic flourish, he handed a blank check to Dhiraj, saying he would sign it if my brother agreed to drop Belle. When Dhiraj refused, my dad saw it as a complete betrayal, and he vowed never to see or speak to Dhiraj again.

In 1960, as I was about to graduate from high school, South Africa was like a ticking bomb, and everyone I knew was waiting for the inevitable explosion. People can be oppressed for only so long before they rise up, and we were all on tenterhooks knowing that a massive revolt against the Afrikaners, though entirely justified, would be a long and bloody business.

Then, in March, came the infamous Sharpeville Massacre.

The ANC and the Pan Africanist Congress, or PAC, a political party that had broken away from the ANC, had launched a campaign to protest the pass laws, which required blacks to carry passbooks and restricted their movements. On March 21, thousands of protestors marched toward the police station at the black township of Sharpeville, near Johannesburg, intending to surrender themselves for refusing to carry their passbooks. Though the movement's leaders had made it clear that they meant for the demonstration to remain peaceful, the marchers were nonetheless met by a large contingent of heavily armed police and low-flying air force fighter jets.

As the crowd pressed on the police station, a small scuffle broke out, and without warning, a police officer standing on top of an armed vehicle began firing into the crowd. His colleagues followed suit, and within a few minutes, 69 people lay dead and another 180 were seriously wounded, many of them shot in the back as they fled.

When news of the massacre reached Cape Town, thousands of protestors gathered at the Langa Flats bus terminal. Police arrived to break up the crowd, killing three and injuring twenty-six.

At Trafalgar High School, the teachers organized a rally to protest the slaying of innocents, and they asked the students to join in. Dhiraj and I decided to go, defying the objections of our worried, disapproving father. He knew that our teachers' instructions to be peaceful would carry little weight with the police, who might decide to shoot us anyway. As we walked the few miles from our school to the police station downtown, our ranks swelled to what seemed to me to be several hundred marchers, chanting and waving placards, and we sensed the growing tension in the air. Armed police came out with bull-horns, shouting at us in Afrikaans to stop blocking the road, to disperse. We held our ground for a while, knowing that bullets could start flying at any moment, mowing us down even as we fled. But after about an hour, the crowd began to disband, and I trudged home, disgruntled and cynical, certain that nothing had been accomplished.

In the following days, the government responded with typical ruthlessness by tightening the noose on political dissent. The ANC and PAC were banned, and a state of emergency was declared. No government officials or police were ever held responsible for the slaughter. As news outlets around the globe reported on the Sharpeville Massacre and its aftermath, at long last, the rest of world had begun awakening to the inhumanity of the South African government.

But to me, Sharpeville was just another signal that those bastard Afrikaners would stop at nothing to hold on to power. I believed that a terrible war was coming and that the situation was hopeless. I was utterly convinced that South Africa would never change—not in my lifetime—and I both hated and despaired for my native country.

I wanted more than ever to get the hell out. I was growing more and more certain that the only happy future for me lay in the Western world. I yearned for the liberty and opportunity that the West offered and felt the pull of certain ideals that I believed existed in free, democratic nations. I wanted to live in a place where I could speak my mind without fear and pursue a better life without restraint.

five
LEARNING TO DREAM

I WAS SAVVY ENOUGH TO KNOW that education would be the ticket I'd need to leave South Africa. But not just any education would do. The University of Cape Town, or UCT, had an international reputation. It was one of the top institutions of higher learning—indeed, in many rankings, it was considered the best—in all of Africa. A degree from UCT, unlike a diploma from the Indian-only university, could open doors for me abroad—so I decided to apply for admission.

A string of rejections followed. At first I thought I'd pursue my interest in politics by going to law school. I didn't get in. Then I switched gears and decided I'd follow Amrit's example and go to medical school. I was turned down again and was told that I must attend the Indian-only university in Durban, which was eight hundred miles away and considered far inferior academically. It didn't help my cause that my high school grades had been mediocre, but the real problem was undoubtedly my race. As a nonwhite, I needed special permission from the government to attend UCT, and the government was controlled by the Afrikaner-run National Party. What's more, despite its attempts to keep up the appearance of being liberal, the university had grown more racially restrictive than ever through the years of Afrikaner rule. My chances of getting in were dim indeed.

As the rejections piled up and the years ticked by, I was no closer to realizing my burning ambition to live abroad. I was also becoming increasingly isolated. I felt little kinship with the Gujarati community, and my once-tight family unit was dissolving before my eyes. My relationship with my father was as strained and distant as ever; even the births of another son, Naresh, and a daughter, Harsheila, didn't seem to soften him.

I honestly don't know what I would have done if it hadn't been for Bhanu. He offered me sanctuary and let me work in his restaurant in the years after I graduated from high school, when my applications to UCT were repeatedly denied and I struggled to figure out what I was going to do with my life. But I owe him for far more than that. Bhanu, my beloved big brother, with his grandiose plans and unquenchable spirit, taught me to dream.

Oh, the big ideas he had! At night, after the restaurant closed, we would sit at the kitchen table and, over a beer or a glass of wine, imagine all manner of schemes for making it big. One of Bhanu's favorite ideas was to manufacture plastic utensils. Across the street from his restaurant was a plastics manufacturing plant, and so Bhanu thought, *Why couldn't I make this stuff too?* He studied the industry and learned how plastic particles could be purchased in bulk, melted down, and molded in giant machines to make forks, spoons, and knives.

He couldn't have had such a business in South Africa; only whites were allowed to own companies in many industries, plastics included. Another idea he had was to start a security guard firm specializing in protecting Indian-owned businesses and property. But that was another nonstarter, because nonwhites weren't allowed to own guns or to employ whites, who were the only ones permitted to carry arms. Bhanu also thought about forming a business devoted to buying old cars and selling the parts. My contribution to the idea pile included making packets of premeasured washing machine detergent, a concept that, to my surprise, became commonplace years later. I also thought we could make a business out of converting old tires into shoes.

All the ventures we dreamed up would have been difficult, if not impossible, for nonwhites like us to get off the ground in

South Africa. So we'd talk about where we'd go. The United States was a favorite fantasy destination. We loved American culture, particularly the big muscle cars that we'd salivate over when we saw them pictured in the magazines that Bhanu kept on a rack in his restaurant. Sometimes we'd visit the Packard dealership about two miles away just to dream about what it would be like to drive one on the open roads of America. Or sometimes we'd talk about going to Australia, or to Brazil, where some of Bhanu's friends had emigrated. Once we were free of the shackles of apartheid, we knew we'd have the freedom to realize our ambitions.

Day after day, I'd work in Bhanu's restaurant, and I also pulled in some extra money from other menial jobs. I worked for a while in a liquor store in the nearby suburb of Woodstock, manning the checkout counter designated for nonwhites. I was also employed for a time as a driver for a doctor, a nice Jewish man with a Citroen, which I'd use to shuttle him around and pick up patients.

Although Bhanu was just a little more than three years older than me and was my closest confidant, he had also become in many ways the de facto head of our family. Amrit, my brilliant oldest brother, had completed medical school at UCT in 1959, and by 1961, he was doing his surgical training in England. Not long after leaving my father's house, Dhiraj had gone to live with his future wife and was studying to become a pharmacist. With my father busy with his new family, it was Bhanu who organized Sunday picnics and barbecues with friends and family. He never excluded his siblings—not once—always insisting we come along with him to parties and outings. People were always bringing their kids to Bhanu's restaurant and his social gatherings, because he adored children, and they adored him right back. He would bounce babies on his knee and fuss over the older kids, showering them with toys and candy. One time, when he was no more than five years old, our little half brother Naresh left my father's home without telling anyone and walked to Bhanu's place, traversing crowded sidewalks and crossing busy intersections. When Bhanu spotted the little guy coming down the street on his own, he couldn't believe his eyes. Naresh had just wanted to be with his generous and gregarious big brother.

Bhanu was also the one among all my siblings who made the greatest effort to keep our mother's memory alive, always keeping a small Hindu shrine with her photograph and incense in his home.

Despite my comfortable life under Bhanu's roof, I still dreamed of getting a top-flight education and using that as my ticket out of South Africa. But, as the years rolled by and it seemed as if I'd never catch a break, many of the other Indians with whom I'd grown up took perverse pleasure in my failure, calling me a loser and making it abundantly clear that they didn't believe I would ever amount to much of anything. Bhanu told me to pay no attention, and so I tried to shut out all the negative chatter. But I was beginning to realize that nothing would happen for me unless I made it happen. I needed to make my own lucky break.

And then I had an idea.

I had discovered a loophole. At that time, the government would consider a nonwhite for a spot at UCT if the applicant could prove that the requisite courses for his major weren't available elsewhere. So once again, I applied to UCT, but this time I sought a bachelor's degree in human physiology and microbiology, because the classes I would need to complete that major weren't offered at the Indian university. I wrote to UCT and the government explaining as much, and then I held my breath and waited.

I'm not quite sure how or why, but it worked. In 1963, at the age of twenty-one, the little loser Himmet Dajee became one of only two nonwhites in the freshman class seeking a bachelor of science degree at the most prestigious university in all of Africa. The other nonwhite student, a colored guy, dropped out in the second year, leaving me alone in a sea of white privilege.

There remained the problem of how I would pay for college, because my savings from my odd jobs were pretty meager. Bhanu, of course, came through for me. He covered most of my costs, including paying rent on a small apartment not far from his place, where I could live and study without the distractions of the restaurant.

Family members posing in front of the shoe store before Bhanu's wedding. Bhanu, center, holds a coconut to break during the ceremony in a common Hindu ritual that symbolizes smashing the ego and humbling oneself before the gods. His father is on the right. Sister Padma and stepmother Sharda are on the left. The children are half siblings Harsheila and Naresh.

At about this same time, Bhanu married a nice young woman, Anjuli. She was also Indian, but the marriage had not been arranged by the families. Bhanu wouldn't have stood for that; he was determined to make his own choice. Anjuli warmly embraced her new husband's siblings as her own, which was a good thing, because by then, Padma and Hansa had also come to live in Bhanu's home behind the restaurant. My father, urged on by his second wife, had wanted my sisters to quit high school and marry young, but Bhanu had once again stood up for his siblings and insisted that the girls stay in school. He was only in his mid-twenties, but he was taking care of three younger siblings along with his new wife.

Nothing was ever easy in South Africa.

When I began at UCT, the South African government was still brutally suppressing any form of dissent against its racist policies. Mandela was already serving a five-year sentence in a Pretoria jail for leaving the country without a passport and inciting a strike. We all knew the real reason he was locked up was that the Afrikaners were afraid of him—he was leading a growing insurrection movement. But even that sentence wasn't enough; the Afrikaners would stop at nothing to get him and his allies permanently out of their way.

In October 1963, Mandela and ten of his ANC colleagues were put on trial on sabotage and conspiracy charges. The Rivonia Trial, often referred to as "the trial that changed South Africa," was named for the Johannesburg suburb where a hideout for the militant wing of the ANC was located. The trial was a farce that resembled nothing approaching justice, but there was widespread fear that the defendants would be sentenced to death. Among them was an Indian, Ahmed Kathrada, who, like me, was the son of immigrants from Gujarat.

Mandela delivered a stirring statement while on the dock, during which he famously declared, "During my lifetime I have dedicated myself to this struggle of the African people. I have fought against white domination, and I have fought against black domination. I have cherished the ideal of a democratic and free society in which all persons live together in harmony and with equal opportunities. It is an ideal which I hope to live for and to achieve. But if needs be, it is an ideal for which I am prepared to die."

Although he and several other defendants were ultimately found guilty, they were sentenced not to death but to life imprisonment. The news clippings from the trial became another sad entry in my scrapbook. The man who I thought represented the best chance for change in South Africa was locked away in prison on tiny Robben Island, so close to Cape Town that it was clearly visible from the city, yet a world away from the freedom that he had struggled to achieve. For me, the trial was another sign that South Africa was doomed. I could only live a fulfilling, useful life somewhere else.

I had a long way to go along a frustrating path to realize my ambitions. From the moment I entered UCT, many teachers and fellow students made it clear that I was not welcome. I was in my first-year chemistry class one day when the professor called out my name and told me to report to the dean of the Faculty of Science. The meeting lasted all of five minutes. He asked me how I got into UCT. I replied that he had all my documentation in front of him and could see for himself. The dean said he wanted to hear the explanation directly from me. So I told him about my major and that the only way I could take the requisite courses was by attending UCT. He thanked me and sent me on my way.

The next year, the two classes I had cited as my reasons for needing to get into UCT were introduced at the Indian university in Durban. The loophole through which I had squeezed had been knitted shut for all future Indian students.

There were other attempts to exclude me. There was a long-standing tradition in the Physiology Department of an annual exchange with the University of Stellenbosch, an Afrikaner institution that was a bastion of apartheid sentiment. The exchange was intended as a forum for students and professors to present projects and discuss key topics. During my third year, it was Stellenbosch's turn to host. Shortly before the event, the chairman of the Physiology Department told me that I would not be welcome at Stellenbosch and couldn't join the exchange. I was crushed. But a couple of other physiology professors stood up for me. If I couldn't go, they said, no one should, and so they decided to boycott the exchange in protest over my exclusion.

The exchange was cancelled, all because the faculty and students at Stellenbosch couldn't bear to recognize a student of Indian descent as an equal. Angry as that made me, I was also gratified that my professors had the integrity to put themselves on the line to do what was right.

Sometimes the other students would chat me up at school, but once we were outside class, the veil went up and they acted as if they didn't know me. I expected that, but it still tore at me. Did they really believe they were better than me, or were they just toeing the line?

Some students made no effort to conceal their racist views. One student who came from Belgian stock would rant to me that blacks weren't capable of running a country and would ruin the former Belgian colony of Congo. It never occurred to him that, as an ethnic Indian, I sympathized greatly with the blacks, whose native lands had also been ravaged by European colonialism.

Yet not everyone treated me badly. For the first time in my life, I was going to school with white students, and to my surprise, many of them were open-minded and treated me well, particularly the Jewish students. I used to wonder if they felt empathy toward nonwhites like me because Jews had been forced to endure extreme adversity. One Jewish girl used to bring me apples, saying she felt sorry for me and didn't know how I could possibly manage to attend university. I wanted to tell her that I wasn't poor and could afford my own apples, but I kept my mouth shut. She just wanted to be kind, and I thought it best not to seem ungrateful.

Some of the other students actually invited me to their homes, which was shocking. One girl asked me to come over to her house, and the black servants looked dumbstruck when they saw me. Another girl invited me to her birthday party, and when I showed up carrying a bottle of wine as a gift, I couldn't believe the opulence. The house had its own library, and wood everywhere! It was beyond my imagination. When I got home and told Bhanu where I'd been, he worried that I had risked getting into trouble with the law just to go to some white girl's party.

He had good reason for concern. I knew I must be constantly on guard, for even the slightest transgression could have landed me in jail or otherwise prevented me from leaving South Africa. It wouldn't take much. Once, while driving my car, I came to a stop at a red light, where a police officer pulled over, saying that I had been speeding. The accusation was ridiculous—we both knew it—for I had been traveling well below the speed limit. Nevertheless, he looked at me as if I were a hardened criminal. He let me go with a warning, but as I drove away, I was torn between indignation and fear over what could easily have been my undoing.

Distrust of the police ran deep in South Africa among people of color. One day, I was walking with a friend near Bhanu's restaurant, when three thugs attacked us. One of them hit me on the back with a nail-studded plank and stole the records I was carrying. I was lucky that the blow didn't puncture one of my lungs. We didn't bother to call the police, though. We knew that at best they wouldn't have done anything and might have even found some excuse to make more trouble for us. The robbery was a scare, but I just chalked it up to life in South Africa. I still have scars on my back from the nails.

As always, I felt as if I were leading a double life, and I was tormented by it. I studied and studied, knowing that education was my ticket out of South Africa, and yet I couldn't concentrate, couldn't seem to get any traction. I lived in constant fear that either I'd completely blow it and flunk out or I'd get stopped by cops and hauled away.

Of course, this affected my academic performance. In my freshman year, I passed botany and zoology, barely squeaked by in physics, and failed chemistry. I had to spend my entire second year retaking chemistry, which I then managed to pass with a decent grade. My third year was a mixture of marginal success and outright failure, and I spent my fourth year making up my bungled physiology course work. I didn't even bother taking my microbiology exam, because I was certain I would fail it.

But another factor was having a negative effect on my school-work: the duality of my life as a son of immigrants with a different culture and language. It was an issue that had plagued me for as long as I could remember. My father's insistence that we speak

only Gujarati had sometimes made it difficult for me to compre-
hend the nuanced phrasing and precise meaning of complex
questions posed in English on the rigorous exams I had to pass
to get my college degree. I recall in particular one test in which
I completely misinterpreted the intent of a critical essay question,
and so my answer had been off the mark. That single mistake
cost me an entire school year, which I had to repeat.

I didn't flunk out, but I was just barely scraping by. I would
talk it over with Bhanu, telling him that I couldn't understand
why I was doing so badly when I studied so diligently and felt
that I comprehended the material. He'd give me one of his pep
talks, telling me to keep working hard and that I would make
it through. So even after four years of excruciating effort and
finding myself still nowhere near completing all the classes I
needed to graduate, I refused to give up. Seeing how hard I
was struggling, a physiology professor offered to tutor me free of
charge. He said he understood that I was treated differently and
how difficult it was for nonwhites to get ahead, and he wanted to
help. This one act of kindness offered by a young white man who
had absolutely nothing to gain from it made a huge impression
on me. I couldn't allow myself to surrender to my fears.

Another event occurred in 1966 that inspired me to hold on
and not lose heart. Robert Kennedy, the American senator and
brother to slain president John F. Kennedy, came to South Africa,
and on June 6, he delivered his "Day of Affirmation" speech on
the UCT campus. It was a seminal moment for the country, for
President Kennedy had been an icon even in South Africa, and
it was well known that he and his brother had championed civil
rights in the United States. When Robert Kennedy accepted the
progressive National Union of South African Students's invitation to visit, many of us saw it as a watershed moment and a
signal that international pressure would eventually persuade
the Afrikaner government to liberalize. We were hungry for
inspiration, for even the smallest glimmer of hope.

I was keen to hear him speak, and I was fortunate that as a
UCT student, I was able to secure a ticket. On the day of the event,
throngs of people swarmed Jameson Hall, the august site of concerts

and commencement ceremonies. But when Kennedy began to speak, the crowd fell silent. I'll never forget his opening words:

> I come here this evening because of my deep interest and affection for a land settled by the Dutch in the mid-seventeenth century, then taken over by the British, and at last independent; a land in which the native inhabitants were at first subdued, but relations with whom remain a problem to this day; a land which defined itself on a hostile frontier; a land which has tamed rich natural resources through the energetic application of modern technology; a land which was once the importer of slaves, and now must struggle to wipe out the last traces of that former bondage. I refer, of course, to the United States of America.

The crowd roared with approval but then again grew quiet. As Kennedy spoke, I was awed by his eloquence and passion, and for a few moments, I forgot how much I hated my country. I felt as if he had somehow reached into my soul and those of all other South Africans who yearned for freedom, that he understood that all we ever really wanted was to be treated fairly.

"Hand in hand with freedom of speech goes the power to be heard, to share in the decisions of government which shape men's lives," he said.

> Everything that makes man's life worthwhile—family, work, education, a place to rear one's children and a place to rest one's head—all this depends on the decisions of government; all can be swept away by a government which does not heed the demands of its people, and I mean all of its people. Therefore, the essential humanity of man can be protected and preserved only where government must answer not just to the wealthy, not just to those of a particular religion, not just to those of a particular race, but to all of the people.

And later, when he declared that no government should restrict the rights of its citizens "to seek education, or to seek work or opportunity of any kind, so that each man may become all that he is capable of becoming," it seemed as if he was talking directly to me.

The hopefulness that Kennedy's speech engendered didn't last long. The Afrikaners remained as intransigent as ever, continuing to find new means to crack down on anyone and anything they considered a threat to their power and enforcing the Group Areas Act, Immorality Laws, and other racist policies with even greater ferocity. Violence was rampant. Indeed, stabbings were so commonplace that UCT was conducting a study on the incidences. I volunteered to participate by helping doctors clean and dress the wounds at Groote Schuur Hospital.

Just two years after his visit to South Africa, Robert Kennedy was cut down by an assassin's bullet, and much of the youthful idealism that he represented died with him. The bitterness inside me grew as I added yet another heart-wrenching page of news clippings to my scrapbook.

Yet I remained determined to channel my anger into something positive, even as I continued to battle my own demons. In the end, it took me six years to complete all the necessary course work. I had muddled through, enduring racism, my father's disapproval, sneers by my Indian peers, and my own crisis of self-confidence, but I finally passed all my exams, allowing me to graduate with a degree in physiology and microbiology. I had at last won that hard-earned prize.

The next step would be to parlay my diploma into a one-way pass out of South Africa.

six

MEANT TO BE

BY MY FINAL YEAR IN COLLEGE, I had decided exactly what I wanted to do. Like Amrit, I would go to medical school and become a doctor.

In hindsight, it feels as if it was always meant to be. I believed that medicine would gain me entrée to the West, to which I felt increasingly drawn and where I believed my future lay. But my desire was fueled by far more than that. Despite my struggles and setbacks in college, I had discovered that I was fascinated by science, particularly the inner workings of the human body. I hungered to learn more, and I wanted to use my knowledge to save other people from the heartache I had known from losing my mother. I knew I had to work every imaginable angle to crack open a door—to get just one medical school to take a gamble on me.

The people who had known me all my life probably thought I was nuts, that I didn't stand a chance. I wasn't smart like Amrit, my grades certainly weren't great, and it had taken me six years to finish my bachelor of science degree. During my final year at UCT, I had applied to medical schools in England, Scotland, Ireland, and Australia, and once again, the denials began piling up. I decided to give South Africa one last try and applied to UCT's vaunted medical school. Not only was I turned down again but the dean of the Faculty of Medicine took the extra trouble of writing me a letter stating flatly that he didn't think I had a future in medicine.

Even Amrit, sounding very much like my perennially disappointed father, saw no reason to encourage me. When I was struggling to complete my undergraduate studies, he once asked me what I wanted to do with my life. I told him I wanted to become a doctor, and he dismissed me coldly, saying, "Why should we bet on a losing horse?"

I'll never forget those words, which cut me to the core and haunt me still after all these years.

Only Bhanu remained, as always, my staunch champion. *To hell with the rest of them,* I thought. I was resolved to prove my doubters wrong and doubled down on my determination.

But after living all my life with obstacles at every turn, I at last had a few aces to play. The first was my degree from UCT. In the United States, students were required to obtain an undergraduate degree before applying to medical school, but this was not the case in many other countries. Amrit had gone straight into medical school from high school, and the programs in other countries to which I'd applied likewise required no undergraduate training. That meant that my degree from a prestigious institution put me ahead of the game. It showed that I had some expertise in science and had already completed some of the necessary course work.

My other ace was Amrit, my skeptical big brother with the illustrious résumé. After graduating from UCT's medical school, he had done his internship at Somerset Hospital in Cape Town and had trained further at a hospital in Port Elizabeth. Then he headed to England, where he worked at a hospital in Southampton before being accepted into a highly prestigious cardiac surgical training program at Great Ormond Street Hospital in London, one of the world's premier children's hospitals. He did further training in Dublin and had passed the Fellow of Royal College of Surgeons exams both there and in London.

The Royal College of Surgeons is primarily an examining body. With additional sites in Edinburgh and Glasgow, the Royal

College has roots dating back to the fourteenth century, when surgeons and barbers were in the same guild. The Royal College in Ireland was granted its charter in 1784, and in 1810, it moved to the location in central Dublin where it remains today. With the motto of "Consilio Manuque"—"scholarship and dexterity"—it is the only one of the four Royal College institutions that also houses a medical school, and it is well known for its philosophy of promoting diversity and accepting large numbers of foreign students. Whether because of my relationship to Amrit with his sterling credentials, my UCT degree, my foreign status, or a combination of the three, the Royal College of Surgeons in Ireland was the one and only medical school to offer me a spot.

After years of rejection letters that felt like bridges being drawn up around the prison fortress in which I lived, I had finally caught a break. I was one lucky sucker, and I knew it, so I didn't hesitate for an instant. I informed the Royal College of Surgeons in Ireland that I was happy to accept its offer of a seat in the incoming class of fall 1969.

My longed-for exit from South Africa was in sight, but I wasn't out of danger yet. I had graduated from UCT in December 1968 and had to wait until the following September to start in Dublin: nine months during which anything could happen. I was still in South Africa, after all.

I walked on eggshells. Bombings were frequent in South Africa at the time, and the perpetrators were suspected of having a background in science. I knew that I had to toe the line and do absolutely nothing to draw attention to myself, because I still needed permission from the government to leave. I even looked into ways to sneak out of the country should I be denied a passport. But when I told Bhanu, he calmed me down and told me not to do anything stupid and get myself arrested or killed. It would all work out, he told me. He had faith, and he insisted that I have faith too.

By then I had moved with Bhanu, his wife, and my sisters to another home in the Indian-designated township Rylands

Estates. Although the government hadn't yet forced us to leave central Cape Town, we knew that the writing was on the wall. District Six, which was adjacent to our old neighborhood, had been declared a whites-only area in February 1966, and more than fifty thousand nonwhite residents had been removed by force. My father and his second family also moved to Rylands, although he was allowed to keep his business on Sir Lowry Road.

During the months that I waited to leave for medical school, I held down a few jobs. I worked for a time in a lab conducting quantitative and qualitative tests on oil extracted from sunflower seeds, peanuts, and corn. Another man doing the same job didn't have a degree, but he was paid much more than I was, for the sole reason that he was white.

Then something unthinkable happened: I became friends with an Afrikaner. I had answered an ad for a job as a draftsman to help a boatbuilder named Reg Muller construct a new boat. I had no experience, but for some reason, Reg took a shine to me and gave me the job anyway. For the next several months, we toiled away at a warehouse in Constantia, a farming area known mostly for its vineyards. When we weren't working, Reg would invite me to his house, where he would talk about politics, trusting that I wouldn't discuss our conversations and his liberal views with anyone else.

When the boat was ready to be launched, Reg invited me to come with him to the whites-only Cape Town Yacht Club. Obviously, I worried what this bold move might lead to, but Reg was adamant. He said, "Himmet, that's my worry, not yours. Just come with me, walk with me, and they can't touch you."

As I walked through the club, I felt every eye trained on me. I could almost hear the indignant whites thinking, *What the hell is this darkie doing here?* I didn't dare laugh, though by Jove, I wanted to. I knew that in Reg, I had made a friend for life.

Reg introduced me to an intriguing young white woman, a student at UCT who, like Reg, was open-minded about relations with other races. Indeed, she had been thrown out of her home and disowned by her parents, who were enraged that she had taken her black nanny to a whites-only beach. She was living on her own in an apartment, but one day, she asked me to come visit her at her aunt and uncle's home. At first, I said, "No way. I can't go there. That would be playing with fire." But she said not to worry: her aunt and uncle were away, and she would sneak me in through the garage so no one would see me.

I took the chance and accepted her invitation. We were alone together in a bedroom, just sitting on the bed and chatting, yet I couldn't relax. Suddenly I heard a shuffling noise outside the door. I leaped up, my heart nearly bursting through my chest. "What's that?" I demanded. "Oh, don't worry," she told me, "that's just my granduncle, and he's blind."

Blind or not, that was all it took to completely unnerve me. I couldn't settle down, and my heart was racing a hundred miles an hour. So I left, for if we'd been caught, there would have been hell to pay. At the time, a sensational trial was being held and the newspapers were full of it: a white professor had been caught in a compromising position with an Indian student. The cops had followed them and obtained photographic evidence that the pair had violated the so-called Immorality Laws banning sexual relations between whites and nonwhites. They were convicted and received suspended sentences, which, in truth, was lucky for them. Other mixed-race couples had been imprisoned for the same crime—daring to love another human being who just happened to have differently colored skin.

I thought about arranging another rendezvous with the young woman. Reg told me that she really liked me, and he teased me, saying, "She wants to have your babies." But, tempting as it was, I was too close to my goal of leaving South Africa and couldn't afford to pursue a relationship with a white girl. I bitterly conceded to the grotesque reality of my situation and told her that I couldn't see her anymore.

I still had more hoops to jump through before I could leave South Africa, chief of which was obtaining a passport, which was far from a sure thing. Nonwhites who applied for a passport were subject to intense governmental scrutiny, and I knew that my passport application would be treated skeptically. Any statement perceived to be false could result in a denial. I had known several people whose passport applications had been denied, and the government never explained why. When I went for the required interview with the police, I was shaking in my boots. It was more like an interrogation, with the officer glancing repeatedly at my file and firing questions at me about my life and plans. One slip, and I would have been out of luck, so I concealed my trembling and lied through my teeth. I said I planned to come back to South Africa after I finished medical school, which was the answer I assumed would give me the best chance of approval. At the end of the interview, the officer told me that my passport would be sent to me, but I didn't believe him until it arrived in the mail weeks later, in March 1969. Six months and counting until my escape.

I continued to tick off the days, hours, and minutes until my departure in September. I wasn't so self-absorbed that I completely ignored the important events that were occurring all over the world, in particular the Vietnam War, which was much in the news and which I fiercely opposed. Then, on July 20, 1969, the Apollo 11 mission landed on the moon. An estimated 530 million people watched the televised images of astronauts Neil Armstrong and Buzz Aldrin taking their first steps on the moon, but we South Africans weren't among them. I could only listen to the description of this momentous accomplishment on the radio. Television was banned in South Africa as part of the Afrikaners' clampdown on the free flow of information. It took an achievement as significant as man's first footsteps on the moon to create a movement among whites to overturn the ban. It would be another seven years before television was introduced in South Africa, and even then, it was restricted to one government-controlled channel. By then I was living abroad and had marveled at the television broadcasts of six other moon expeditions.

As my time in South Africa grew shorter, I knew that Bhanu was happy for me, yet I also sensed that his feelings were bittersweet.

I was leaving, and he would be left behind. He didn't complain about it; he never would have burdened me with his own disappointments. He was a dreamer, true, but he was also a realist and knew that without even a high school diploma, his options were limited. What's more, by the time I left, he had started another business, which sold clothing, shoes, and hats. A significant part of his sales consisted of school uniforms, and he was busy filling the many contracts he had secured with local nonwhite schools. He also had to think of his wife and how the monumental choice to uproot their lives to move abroad would affect her. They had no children—they had tried desperately but without success to start a family—and his sadness over that must have weighed heavily on him. In short, he had plenty on his mind beyond his little brother's impending departure.

As for me, as the day grew closer, I refused to allow any doubt to creep in. I had decided that the only way I could live my life from the moment I left South Africa would be never to look back, to keep pushing ahead toward a destiny that I would create for myself. I was convinced that if I stuck to that philosophy, I could achieve my goals and escape my tormented past. Even the prospect of leaving Bhanu couldn't shake me from this conviction. For years, I had been like a tripod with one broken leg, and only his support had kept me balanced. Although I owed him so much, and loved him dearly, I couldn't afford the distraction of even the tiniest of misgivings.

So I pushed aside all traces of regret or sadness and focused only on the future of freedom and happiness that I envisioned. One day, Bhanu would join me in my new life, and he could at last pursue one of his many business ideas. Until then—well, I was leaving, that was that, and I could barely contain my elation that I was finally getting the hell out of South Africa. And so I said my good-byes to Bhanu and the rest of my family. No regrets, I told myself. Keep moving forward. Never look back.

On the day I left, September 15, 1969, I flew from Cape Town to Johannesburg, my first time on an airplane. As my international flight took off from Johannesburg en route to Frankfurt and then London, where I had arranged to spend a few days before heading to Dublin, I could almost feel myself willing the plane off the ground. My body felt lighter and my mind began racing as we soared higher and faster.

We weren't even a half hour into the flight when the captain announced that we had engine trouble and had to return to Johannesburg. I went into a mad panic, imagining the worst scenario: that I would be denied permission to board another plane. That's how much I mistrusted the authorities in South Africa.

But the next day, I was back on another flight and on my way to begin my new life. I was twenty-seven years old, and I was just beginning to know what it meant to feel free.

Keep moving forward. Never look back.

seven

ALL UP TO ME

BEFORE MY LIFE IN A NEW WORLD COULD BEGIN, my father had insisted that I undertake a very old world task. During my few days in London, he wanted me to meet with an Indian man whom he thought would make a good husband for my sister Padma.

I was reluctant, to say the least. I knew very well that neither of my sisters wanted an arranged marriage, but I agreed to meet the guy just to keep the peace with my father. I quickly discovered that his choice for a son-in-law was a shallow playboy and wrote to my dad that there was no way I'd let my sister anywhere near him.

I'm not sure I can adequately describe the feelings that overwhelmed me when I first set foot in Dublin. Elation. Relief. Fulfillment. Vindication. For the first time in my life, I felt no constraints, nothing to hold me back from my hopes and dreams. I suppose anyone who has lived through oppression would understand how momentous it is to taste the sweetness of freedom for the first time. Although I wasn't religious, I felt an almost spiritual exultation.

I hadn't gotten there on my own; I was well aware of that. I'd had lots of help along the way, especially from my brothers. Indeed, Amrit had seemingly overcome his skepticism about my chances for success and had gone to great lengths to support me. By then, he had moved to the United States, where he was a general surgical resident at Temple University's Albert Einstein Medical Center in Philadelphia. But he flew to Ireland to meet me at the airport along with a family with whom he had arranged for me to live while I attended medical school—the same people with whom he had boarded during his time in Dublin.

He couldn't have set up a better situation for me. My landlords, Ruth and Ivan Farrar, and their two young children welcomed me into their home with open arms. I was a complete stranger, a skinny, dark-skinned Indian raised in the Hindu faith in an African country—about as far as anyone could have been from the jovial, fair-complexioned Irish. Yet, from the moment I entered the Farrars' home in Dublin, I felt enveloped in their warmth and unconditional acceptance. Ruth and Ivan were only about ten years older than me, but they treated me with an almost parental affection. As I settled into a spare room fashioned from the attached garage in their comfortable, two-story house, I began to experience a lightness and contentment I'd never known before, and I thought, *I've arrived. I've finally arrived.*

I got another big break. Because I had earned an undergraduate degree from UCT, I was allowed to take a test to qualify for two open spots in the second-year class. If I passed, I would graduate from medical school in five years instead of six, and given that I was already older than the other students, I badly wanted that edge.

During the oral examination, I was grilled about the Krebs cycle, the properties of various chemicals, and all manner of scientific processes. The answers flowed out of me absolutely perfect, and I passed easily. It was only my first week at the Royal College, but already I had the unaccustomed feeling of being valued and respected. It was a completely new sensation, and I reveled in it.

Yet I really wasn't studying more or working any harder than I had as an undergraduate. The difference was that now everything just felt right. I believed I was finally where I was supposed to be, doing what I was meant to do, and I was treated as an equal. About half of the other students were foreigners too. They came from all over the world—Scandinavia, the United States, Canada, Australia, Ghana, Nigeria, Malaysia—yet we quickly formed a cohesive group with a common mission. I felt at home in my new community, and as a result, something inside me clicked satisfyingly into place.

Not that I was in any position to take my good fortune for granted. This was the opportunity, the door to my future I had fought so long and hard to pry open. My brothers had helped me get to this point. Now it was all up to me, and I'd have to work like the dickens to prove that their support hadn't been wasted. Failure would mean I'd have to return to South Africa, and that was unthinkable.

My transformation was instantaneous. The barely average kid who squeaked by throughout grade school, high school, and college, the underachieving young man who was branded a loser by his peers back in South Africa, suddenly began to flourish. I was focused, assertive, and confident in my abilities. Anyone who goes to medical school must be ambitious and dedicated, and the competition is intense, but even among the other students, I soon became known for my fierce drive and hunger for success.

My body freed from the shackles I had known under apartheid, my mind became unshackled as well. I devoured all the assigned books and materials and stood out in class for my inquisitiveness and quick comprehension. I prepared for whatever was coming next by reading ahead so I would know what to expect and where I might need help. My books looked far from virginal; I scribbled notes in the columns, underlined important passages, and dog-eared page after page as a reminder to review critical material.

In my first year, among a class of one hundred students, I quickly distinguished myself as one of the best. I was in the top three or four in every class—anatomy, biochemistry, physiology—and began winning the first of what would be many honors and medals for academic excellence.

My life in Ireland was blessedly simple, focused, and rewarding. I spent most of my time at school or at home studying in my bedroom. Amrit left his Fiat 500 for me, and I used it to drive the four miles to the Royal College, which was housed in an elegant, columned structure built in the early nineteenth century on St. Stephen's Green in the center of Dublin. In my precious spare time, I also used my little car to tool around the country. I went for weekend outings in the luxuriously green countryside of Wicklow and Waterford and loved strolling around the city, stopping by Trinity University to see the Book of Kells or just to sit and gaze at the pretty girls. I wandered into majestic old cathedrals like St. Patrick's and Christ Church, where I planted myself in a pew and listened to the soothing organ recitals, which sounded far more pleasing to my ear than the clanging, discordant Indian music my father loved. I also indulged in occasional nights at the theater and attended a few anti-apartheid lectures at Trinity.

My adopted family, the kindly Farrars, included me in every meal and outing, and it didn't take long for me to become friends with their large extended family too. Ivan managed a laundry facility, and Ruth was a stay-at-home mom, a warmhearted soul who played the piano brilliantly. Her father, a lovely, gentlemanly man whom I got to know quite well, managed a shoe store—my connection to shoes seemed fated as well—on Grafton Street, a short walk from the Royal College, and I'd often visit him on my lunch breaks or sip coffee at Bewley's Cafe, across from his shop.

Ruth and Ivan were something of an anomaly in Ireland, as they weren't Catholic or even mainstream Protestant. They were Brethrens, a Christian faith that emphasizes the New Testament and embraces principles of peace, nonmaterialism, and compassion. They didn't push their religion on me, but I sometimes enjoyed accompanying them to their church services, which I found calming.

I was well aware that Ireland had its own torturous history of religious strife and subjugation under British rule, and I'd sometimes read about bombings in Northern Ireland and the occasional spillover of troubles into the south. Yet for me, it was a place of tranquility after my conflicted upbringing. I never once sensed any feeling of antagonism toward me, an outsider, or witnessed any hint of violence. The weather was dreary as hell—that was my only complaint—so the garrulous natives spent much of their leisure time either at church or at their local pub. Indeed, one of my first observations about my new home was that virtually every street had a church on one corner and a pub on the other. It was a very practical arrangement.

Much as I enjoyed exploring Ireland, I knew I mustn't get sidetracked in any way from my objective. But I didn't mind that I often had to forgo parties and outings for my studies. Not only did I appreciate the opportunity I'd been given but I found that I was truly fascinated by the inner workings of the human body: its chemical and biological processes, the interaction of the organ systems, the intriguing interconnectedness of everything. I dove into my first-year classes with gusto, consuming every bit of information I could get my hands on. At the beginning of my first year, I approached *Cunningham's Textbook of Anatomy* and *Gray's Anatomy* with trepidation, thinking they'd be excruciating to get through, but by the end, I had absorbed every word of the massive textbooks. I learned all the details of each nerve, vein, artery, and branch; the intricate physiology of the ear, nose, and tongue; and how sensory information is transmitted to and interpreted by the brain.

A rite of passage for medical students is the first visit to the cadaver lab. As we filed in, I was instantly assailed by the aggressively pungent stench of formalin. Then I saw the bodies, about twenty-five of them, lined up on tables and covered in moist cloth. I flashed back momentarily to South Africa and the absurdity of UCT rules dictating that any nonwhite student who participated in autopsies on white bodies would be summarily expelled. We split up into groups of four to begin dissecting, learning about each part of the body as we went. Here, for once, my humble background of chopping up chickens and working with leather might have given me an edge, or at least a level of comfort with the cold, hard cadavers that some of my classmates might not have shared.

Exams, both oral and written, were meticulous. We would be asked to describe the distribution of facial nerves with precision and in detail, for instance, or to describe how the sympathetic nervous system traverses the spine. We had to know not only the pathway of every nerve, artery, and vein but also what was on top of, below, and to the right and left of each. I admired the professors immensely, but I wasn't intimidated. *If they can do it, I can do it,* I told myself. *One day, I'm going to be one of these guys.*

On the day grades were posted, the students thronged the corridors to search for their names on the boards, and a shout went up whenever someone spotted his and learned he had passed. Deep in my heart, I knew I had done well, and when I saw my scores, among the top in every class, I felt redeemed. I wasn't the dumb guy I used to be in South Africa. Now I was one of the best. Afterward, of course, we all went to a pub for a drink.

But I encountered a critical snag during my first year, when my father informed me that he was no longer willing to pay my expenses. He offered no explanation or apology; he just informed me of his decision and suggested, "Go ask your brothers." It was like a sock to the gut. The father who had pontificated ad nauseam to his children about the importance of education was leaving me high and dry just as I was finally experiencing some success—decades later, I learned that my dad's withdrawal was meant as my punishment for refusing to submit to an arranged marriage—but fortunately, I had applied for and received a scholarship from the United Nations Educational, Scientific, and Cultural Organization, UNESCO, reserved for students who had been subjected to discrimination under apartheid. But that covered my tuition only; I still needed help to pay for my room and board.

Once again, one of my brothers came to my rescue. Amrit, impressed with my first-year grades and now taking my ambitions seriously, agreed to foot the bill for the remainder of medical school. And again, I was grateful beyond measure. But my complicated, tortured relationship with my father had taken another turn for the worse, and we had little contact for some time after. My frequent letters home were reserved for my brothers and sisters, and they wrote back with news about our family and friends and their fears about the escalating violence in South Africa.

I didn't dwell on my family situation, not even on my lingering hope that Bhanu would join me once I settled into my career somewhere in the West. I had no time or inclination to think about anything other than the task at hand: continuing to excel in medical school. I didn't even return home to visit during summer 1970, after I'd completed my first year at the Royal College, opting instead to stay in Dublin and spend part of my time traveling around England and Scotland. I saw the Royal Tattoo at Edinburgh Castle, took in a Shakespearean play in Stratford-upon-Avon, and got goose bumps as I walked in the steps of Sir Isaac Newton at Oxford University. I was fascinated by the sense of history that permeated the British Isles and loved gawking at the centuries-old buildings and majestic castles.

In the years that followed, I proved that my first-year success was not a fluke. As I continued on in my course work, I studied psychology, pathology, pharmacology, anesthetics, pathology, more physiology, ophthalmology, otorhinolaryngology, medicine, surgery, forensic medicine, toxicology, psychiatry, pediatrics, obstetrics and gynecology, and social and preventive medicine. And every year, I racked up more honors and medals. I even boasted a picture in the *Irish Medical Times* with a pathology professor and two other students who had also won medals.

From the beginning of medical school, I realized that if I truly wanted to distinguish myself, even the very best grades wouldn't be enough, and I determined to burnish my résumé in any way possible. So in summer 1971, after my second year at the Royal College in Dublin, I decided to pursue a concurrent medical degree from the University of London through its external program. Every year, after taking my exams in Dublin, I'd fly to London and take the required exams there. I stayed at the International House, a dormitory for students coming from all over the world. I was a little nervous at first, but as the written and oral exams commenced, I realized that the Royal College had prepared me well. To my surprise, I breezed confidently through the London exams, and I knew I had made the right decision in choosing to pursue another degree.

The summer after my second year of medical school, following my London exams, I applied for and was accepted to a prestigious surgical elective at Westminster Hospital, which was affiliated with the University of London. Although anatomy is a notoriously dry subject, one of the surgeons at Westminster, Harold Ellis, had written an engaging book on anatomy that clearly explained how to use all that technical information we learned in school to diagnose and treat patients. I knew that the experience of training under him would be invaluable. For two months, I shadowed Dr. Ellis and the surgical fellows, doing rounds with them; taking patients' clinical histories; and being grilled by the senior physicians with their questions about diagnoses, recommended tests, and courses of treatment. I observed operations as surgeons gave detailed explanations of their methods while they worked.

During my stay in London that summer, I began dating a Welsh girl, another medical student whom I had met at Westminster Hospital. She was sweet, but I was too busy to commit to a long-term relationship, and she admitted to me that if her parents found out she was seeing a nonwhite, they'd hit the roof. She told me they called my kind "golliwogs." It was the first time I heard that term, but I assumed it wasn't flattering. I'd had more than my fill of racism in South Africa, and I wasn't about to knowingly expose myself to more of it.

The following summer, after my second set of London exams, I visited Amrit in Philadelphia. I had been eager to see the United States, but my first impression of the country was rather bleak. The medical center where Amrit was a general surgical resident was in a high-crime area. During my stay, I heard reports that a medical student had been stabbed to death, and Amrit's friends told stories about parked cars stripped of their hubcaps and even of their tires. I wondered privately why Amrit would want to live in a hellish place like that.

But as I began to explore, my view changed. So many places and images stand out in my mind from that trip, starting in Philadelphia with the Liberty Bell, which made me yearn for a revolution in my native country. I also made a point of seeing Jefferson Medical School, where, in 1953, an American surgeon named John Heysham Gibbon Jr. had invented the revolutionary heart-lung machine. I felt as awestruck as I had when I was in Oxford.

I spent a few days with Amrit, and then I embarked on a solo, monthlong cross-country trip. Traveling on Greyhound buses, I visited Baltimore, Washington, D.C., Chicago, Denver, Salt Lake City, San Francisco, Los Angeles, Las Vegas, Phoenix, Tucson, El Paso, San Antonio, Houston, New Orleans, and Atlanta, and then moved on to Toronto, Montreal, and Boston. I spent no more than one or two days in each city before climbing back aboard another bus. I met hundreds of people, who were almost uniformly friendly, chatty, and completely mystified by my strange accent.

The vastness of the country was stunning. I'd gaze out the window as we traversed huge swaths of land, crossing mountain ranges, endless prairies, and fields of crops that stretched for miles and miles. Even the ubiquitous billboards were more grandiose than other billboards I'd seen. The air conditioning on the buses was always cranked up to high, and the moment I stepped off a bus to look around, I was smote with suffocating heat. But I was determined to see all the sights, from the Lincoln Memorial in Washington, D.C., to Fisherman's Wharf in San Francisco. I recall the leathery smell of cowboy boots in Denver, which reminded me of home; the pin-drop acoustics of the Mormon Tabernacle in Salt Lake City; the vibrant gaudiness of the Sunset Strip in Los Angeles; and the wrought iron balconies and jazz music of New Orleans's French Quarter. I visited many medical institutions along the way, including the Baylor College of Medicine in Houston, made world famous by the brilliant Dr. Michael DeBakey because of his innovations in heart surgery.

By the time I flew back to Dublin to resume my medical studies, I'd realized that my picture of the United States had changed. Although I had long imagined that I might eventually settle and start a practice in America, I'll admit to having had conflicted and sometimes negative feelings about the country. This was 1972, and it was a tumultuous time. The Vietnam War was in full swing, the Watergate scandal had just broken, and with the *Roe v. Wade* Supreme Court decision a year away, the abortion debate was raging. My opinion of the United States was also influenced by the country's own history of racism and by the government's tacit support of apartheid (the latter fueled by the unjustified fear that if the Afrikaners fell from power, South Africa would be overrun by communists). But my long journey, which had allowed me to experience so much beauty and meet so many kind and interesting people, gave me a deeper perspective from which to consider this diverse, complicated, and undeniably awe-inspiring nation.

The next year, after my summer exams in London, I returned to the United States, but this time I had a different purpose. One of my favorite professors, Harold Browne, had suggested that I apply for a general surgical elective at the world-famous Mayo Clinic in Rochester, Minnesota. Professor Browne was an impressive man. A perfectionist and rigid taskmaster, he had once scolded me for touching an overhead light in an operating room. The light wasn't sterile, he reminded me, and he sent me back out to scrub up again. It was a lesson I never forgot. But he also had a wonderfully dry sense of humor, and for some reason, he had decided to take me under his wing. He had done part of his training at the Mayo Clinic, and I have no doubt his recommendation helped me secure a highly coveted spot in the two-month program.

At the Mayo Clinic, I worked under the surgical staff, going on rounds, taking patient histories, conducting examinations, reviewing lab work, making diagnoses, and suggesting courses of treatment. I observed operations as surgeons explained step-by-step what they were doing and why. It was terrific hands-on training, although I couldn't help noticing that the American system placed less emphasis on examining and talking to patients and a greater reliance on tests. To my mind, it was confirmation that I was receiving the very best education at the Royal College.

During my short time at the Mayo Clinic, I encountered a famous patient, Dean Rusk, who had served as secretary of state under Presidents Kennedy and Johnson. He'd had surgery to repair an abdominal aneurysm, and when I checked in on him during rounds, he asked me if the surgeons had had the opportunity to check out his heart during the operation. I explained to him that this would not have been possible, because the chest organs are separated from the abdomen by the diaphragm.

eight

MY CALLING

I HADN'T YET DECIDED CONCLUSIVELY what type of medicine I wanted to practice, but as I progressed through medical school, the picture became clearer. Some specialties didn't appeal to me at all. I won a silver medal for academic excellence in psychiatry, even though I hated the subject, because it felt less concrete than other disciplines and the trips we made to a mental institution disturbed me. By contrast, the intricate yet precise and relatively unambiguous subjects of anatomy and physiology were among my favorites. In my second year, we began visiting the morgue, which was even tougher for some of my classmates to stomach than the cadaver lab, because this time we were working with fresh corpses. Blood oozed out when the professor began cutting into a body to open the sternum and show us the organs below, and the guy standing next to me passed out cold on the floor. I, however, wasn't just unfazed; I was fascinated. I hadn't decided for certain, but deep down I think I knew early on that I was inching my way toward choosing surgery.

It wasn't because Amrit was a surgeon—or at least mostly it wasn't. In part, my interest was a natural consequence of my education at the Royal College of Surgeons, which, as its name implies, leaned heavily toward producing surgeons. But most significantly, I was drawn to surgery because a fire had been kindled in me and burned ever brighter as I learned more and more about the beautiful, almost mystical way that all the intricate systems within the human body worked together. A surgeon's job requires a deep understanding and appreciation of that elaborate interior network, and I found that challenge almost seductively alluring. Surgery appealed to my practical nature too. When something went wrong, a surgeon could reach inside and take concrete steps to make it right. I was increasingly confident that I had the intellectual chops, cool head, and steady hands required of someone willing to cut deep into a person, peeling back layers of skin and tissue to find and repair a problem, and then get back out again without causing more damage. My confidence, once in short supply, was soaring, and the thought of many more years of difficult study and training didn't intimidate me a bit.

Also like Amrit, I felt myself increasingly gravitating toward cardiothoracic surgery, a highly elite specialty that deals with chest organs, primarily the heart and lungs. In large measure, I was drawn to cardiothoracic because my mother's doomed battle with her asthmatic lungs was always in the back of my mind.

A sad loss toward the end of my stay in Ireland also had a big impact on my direction. Ruth's father, an absolute gentleman with whom I had become close, had a history of angina and had been taking nitroglycerin under his tongue to treat it. One day, he began experiencing severe chest pain. I met the family at the hospital, and I was dismayed by the almost bumbling attempts to save him, which ultimately proved futile. In those days, options for heart patients were far more limited than they are today. People with symptoms were often just put to bed and given intravenous pain medication. Bypass surgery—a method of replacing damaged arteries in the heart with blood vessels from another part of the body—had recently been introduced in Ireland, but it was hardly commonplace at the time. I acted as the liaison between the hospital staff and the family and broke the awful news to Ruth and her mother. I'll never forget the sense of helplessness and defeat I felt as I witnessed their grief. *Why do people have to die?* I asked myself. *We can do better. I want to do better.*

At the funeral, I managed a calm exterior, but inside I was overcome with emotion. Perhaps the service reminded me of my mother. It was a different religion with unfamiliar rituals, but it didn't matter—the feelings were the same. Death is death. Whether the body is buried or cremated, it turns to dust. The person you loved is gone, and only the memories and the pain remain.

I knew for certain then that more than anything in the world, I wanted to save people. White skin, black, brown, it made no difference. Under that thin epidermis, we all have the same organs and vessels. If something went wrong, I wanted to be the one to delve deep inside and fix it. I couldn't remember a time when I hadn't been angry, but now I was in a position to channel that anger into something meaningful. I had found my calling.

It was June 1974. I had worked my tail off for five years and passed all the necessary exams. Wearing my rented cap and gown, I stood inside the large hall on the second floor of the Royal College of Surgeons of Ireland and recited the Hippocratic Oath as Amrit, who had flown over from America, and Ruth watched. I heard my name called and marched up to receive my diploma. For the very first time, I heard the magnificent words that would open up a new world of possibilities for me: "Dr. Himmet Dajee."

Before I began the next phase of my career, I decided that I would finally return to South Africa to see my family. Save for my visits with Amrit, I hadn't seen any of my siblings or my father since I'd left for medical school five years before. Even so, I was going back with mixed feelings. I was anxious to see Dhiraj, Hansa, Padma, and especially Bhanu. But I was annoyed because my father and Amrit were pressuring me to move back to South Africa permanently to practice medicine there—and that was a notion I couldn't abide.

"You can't abandon your family and the community," Amrit would say, to which I replied, "To hell with the community. The community thought I was an idiot."

The sad truth is that Amrit had wanted badly to return himself, and it was a source of bitterness and regret to him that he hadn't been able to. Indeed, the way he was treated was a travesty. Here was a brilliant surgeon with a prestigious double fellowship who had been trained in, and worked at, some of the world's premier medical institutions. He should have been welcomed with open arms anywhere he chose to practice. But in apartheid South Africa, merit and accomplishment meant nothing if the person applying for a position wasn't white.

He had contacted other cardiac surgeons working in South Africa—all white, of course—asking if there were any opportunities available for him there. Among those with whom he corresponded was Christiaan Barnard, a rock star among cardiothoracic surgeons, renowned throughout the world for performing the first human heart transplant in 1967 at Groote Schuur Hospital in Cape Town. Barnard, chairman of the UCT Medical School's Department of Cardiothoracic Surgery, had cultivated a reputation as a progressive. He had spoken out against apartheid, was known to ignore racial barriers by sometimes allowing mixed-race nurses to treat white patients, and had transplanted hearts from white people into nonwhite patients.

Amrit also appealed to Barnard's boss, Jannie Louw, chairman of surgery at UCT Medical School. He had hoped, naively perhaps, that Barnard and Louw would welcome the opportunity to make another kind of history by hiring South Africa's first nonwhite cardiothoracic surgeon. He even assured them that he would confine his work to nonwhite patients and use exclusively nonwhite bodies when performing dissections in anatomy classes.

Not one of Amrit's attempts to reach out to these surgeons resulted even in an interview, let alone a job offer. Barnard and Louw gave him some bullshit answers about there being no opportunities for him there, but in their letters, which Amrit showed me, I could read between the lines. Many times in South Africa, I had seen whites profess their opposition to apartheid, but then, when it came down to it, they lacked the courage of their convictions. I felt certain that despite Barnard's liberal reputation, he and his boss didn't want to deal with the backlash that would ensue if they gave a nonwhite—no matter how well qualified—such a prestigious position.

Amrit made many other attempts to find a good surgical post in South Africa, but all of them backfired. No hospital in Cape Town would take him, and it was made clear that even if he did find a spot, he would earn only a fraction of a white doctor's salary. He was cut to the quick by the repeated denials, but that didn't stop him from inviting Barnard to speak at Brown University's Rhode Island Hospital, where Amrit was then doing two years of cardiothoracic surgical residency training, an invitation that Barnard—never one to shy away from the limelight—had been all too happy to accept.

I was furious and accused Amrit of flattering Barnard in another futile effort to get him to open a few doors.

"Why do you want to go back?" I demanded. "These guys don't like us. We'll never get anywhere in South Africa. Be happy. You're overseas; you're doing fine." Amrit just shrugged. But I could see that the rejection was taking a toll on him.

Perhaps that was what prompted Amrit to set his sights on convincing me that I should be the one to go back and serve as a general physician in my local community—likely the only position that would have been open to me in South Africa. But I refused to consider it, refused to live and work under these or any other humiliating conditions. I wanted to keep moving forward. "I've done all this to get out of South Africa," I told Amrit. "Why would I want to go back? Apartheid is still there. It hasn't changed." He wasn't happy with my response, but I was adamant.

So when I returned to Cape Town after graduating from medical school, a newly minted doctor, I made it clear to everyone that I would stay only for a few weeks. I had already accepted the Royal College's offer of a one-year internship. And upon my return to Dublin, I planned to begin applying to other programs for the year after.

If I'd had any lingering doubts about my decision, my father's reaction upon my return dispelled them. My dad, the same man who had refused to help me after my first semester in medical school, the man who shut out his children after our mother's death and his remarriage, suddenly couldn't get enough of me. All he wanted to do during my visit was shuttle me around to see his friends and brag about his son the doctor. I felt as if he was taking credit for my success, and I wanted to explode. He further ticked me off by pestering me again to get married to an Indian girl.

Many of the guys in my age group—the ones who used to call me a loser and tell me that I might as well give up because I'd never amount to anything—were just as bad. Now that I was a doctor, they were fawning all over me, and I found their obsequiousness just as offensive as their put-downs had been. I said nothing to them, or to my father. My past failures had been part of my journey, and now that I was at last experiencing some happiness and fulfillment, I refused to let bitterness and spite over my old life bog me down. At least that's what I told myself.

After five years away, I was alarmed by the worsening conditions in South Africa. As anti-apartheid unrest grew, the government responded in a horribly predictable way: by tightening the screws on nonwhites. There had been more forcible evictions, more people herded into crowded, miserable townships. The fear over escalating violence was evident; crime was commonplace. The contrast with my peaceful life in Ireland was shocking.

By that time, Dhiraj was working as a pharmacist, and he and Belle lived with their three young children in Cape Town. My father, stubborn as ever, still refused to accept their marriage, but as far as I could see, my brother and his wife were happy and getting along just fine without his approval.

Padma was doing secretarial work, and Hansa had a job as a technician at the Red Cross Children's Hospital blood bank transfusion lab. They were both still living with Bhanu and Anjuli, and still resisting my father's attempts to arrange marriages for them.

The best part of my trip, of course, was that now, after five years apart, I could once again spend time with Bhanu. He too asked me if I might consider moving back to South Africa to work as a general practitioner. But with Bhanu, I always knew that his heart was in the right place. He missed me, as I missed him, and he wanted us to be together again. I told him that I hadn't changed my mind, that I didn't belong in South Africa anymore. "This place will never change," I said. There was no way I'd come back, and I was determined to keep moving ahead and do my surgical training abroad. He didn't pressure me, didn't try to make me feel guilty—that wasn't his way—yet I sensed a hint of sadness in his subdued demeanor.

So we discussed what he might do. I badly wanted to share my new freedom with him, and I pushed him to get out of South Africa too, to begin making plans to join me overseas as soon as possible. But for him, leaving South Africa would be fraught with obstacles. His clothing business was fairly successful, but it could have been taken away from him at any moment, and all that he had invested in it would have been lost. He was in a tricky situation, because he had established the business in Retreat, a colored-only area. So he had made a backdoor arrangement with some partners who were colored, which allowed him to continue operating there. If they had been discovered, Bhanu could have lost everything and possibly even been charged with a crime. Extricating himself from these business dealings would take some doing. There was also the question of finding a means to support himself and Anjuli in a foreign country. Bhanu, ever the protector, felt responsible for Padma and Hansa too, and he wanted to make sure that whatever decisions he made, they would also be provided for.

Despite Bhanu's naturally optimistic nature, I could tell that these issues troubled him, as did his great disappointment that he and Anjuli were unable to have children. I think perhaps in a way he was envious of me—not jealous, but yearning and some-what frustrated that he was still struggling to find his own path and live up to his full potential. "We're not going to be together again," he said just before I left. But I refused to believe it. Amrit was in the United States, and I too would likely end up there eventually. "Come on, just get out," I insisted, and I promised that I would look for opportunities for him abroad. He agreed that he would come just as soon as he could.

Soon, very soon, I hoped, we would be together again.

Upon my return to Ireland, I immersed myself in my internship, and in my applications for the following year, pushing my concerns about South Africa and my family to the back of my mind. I was completely independent financially for the first time in my life, and I saw only blue sky and open roads ahead.

My last year in Dublin went quickly. I spent the first three months doing a neurosurgical rotation and was surprised by the primitive state of that specialty at the time. Back then, it was still difficult to distinguish between malignancies and healthy tissue, so often during surgery normal brain tissue was sucked out along with the tumors. Too many patients suffered some form of permanent neurological damage, and this distressed me.

Next I was assigned to my old medical school mentor, Dr. Harold Browne, for a rotation in general surgery, which typically involved operations in the abdomen. I also received training in vascular surgery, a specialty focused on repairing damaged arteries and veins, and in orthopedic surgery. I assisted in operating rooms, helped monitor pre- and postoperative care, checked on test results, watched vital signs, drew blood, and learned to suture.

I experienced a first during that year—one that every doctor would like to avoid but ultimately must face: I watched a patient die. What made it even more horrible was that he was just a little boy, seven, perhaps eight years old. He'd been run over by a car, which ravaged his pancreas, releasing toxic juices into his body that were eating away at his other organs. A pancreatic leak is always big trouble, and there was little we could do. We gave him liquid nutrition through a tube inserted into a large vein in his neck to give his bowel and pancreas a rest in the hope that the leak would seal off. But it was hopeless. We filled him with pain medication, and I stayed with him until the end, watching as his little face transformed from clenched agony to serene repose when his heart ceased to beat. I was gutted.

Another first-time experience was equally traumatic. One night during my neurosurgical rotation, I assisted a doctor who tried desperately to save a young man—he couldn't have been older than about twenty—who had been in a motorcycle accident and suffered severe brain damage. There was nothing more to be done. There was no brain activity; he was technically dead, so the lead surgeon instructed me to remove the endotracheal tube connected to the ventilator that had been keeping the patient oxygenated. I hesitated. *Why me?* I thought. *Why do I have to pull the plug?* I'd never done such a thing before, and I was overwhelmed with a sense of defeat. I wanted to save people, not watch helplessly as they breathed their last. But I also knew that making difficult decisions and taking responsibility were part of the job. So I did it. But I never forgot. And I swore that if I could help it, no death would be in vain, for each one could teach me something that I might use to save another patient. It is not by accident that many medical advancements have been birthed in tragedy.

My final months in Ireland were mostly devoted to figuring out where I'd go next. I was still harboring conflicted and sometimes negative feelings about the political situation in the United States, and even though I wanted to live there eventually, I saw Canada as a good choice in the interim. But I had another reason for seeking a position in Canada, one that would prove to offer a critical advantage in my career—and that might not have occurred to me had it not been for Amrit.

My brilliant big brother had encountered a serious roadblock when he moved from England to the United States. One of his motivations for going to America in the first place was that, as a surgeon, more doors would be open to foreigners like him, whereas in Britain at that time, getting to the top—a *consultancy* is the term used there—was extremely rare for nonnatives. But there was a hitch, and it was a doozy. The American system, it turned out, didn't recognize Amrit's previous surgical training. So there he was with a prestigious dual fellowship in surgery, and he had to do it all over again. He was forced to repeat six years of intensive training to earn the proper credentials to work as a cardiothoracic surgeon in the United States.

But strangely enough, I learned that no such restriction was placed on Canadian-trained surgeons. By doing my surgical residency in Canada, I could avoid Amrit's dilemma and, if I did well, move seamlessly into the U.S. system without having to repeat any of my training. Without even trying this time, Amrit had once again helped me out. Unfortunately, his assistance had come in the form of showing me what *not* to do.

Though he was intensely bitter about his situation, Amrit was nonetheless annoyed with my decision to apply only to programs in Canada. I decided to accept an offer to do a one-year surgical and medical internship at Dalhousie University in Halifax, Nova Scotia. After that, I would apply for surgical residency programs, but for now, I told myself, one step at a time.

"I've never heard of this place," Amrit grumbled. No matter. I was thrilled. Dalhousie University had a long and storied history. It was founded in 1818 and named after George Ramsey, the ninth Earl of Dalhousie and lieutenant governor of Nova Scotia at the time, who modeled the school after the University of Edinburgh, near his own ancestral Scottish home. "Nova Scotia" is the Latin equivalent of "New Scotland," and though I'd yet to see it, the blending of the Old World with the New appealed to me. Another bonus would be that Amrit, who was still at Brown University in Rhode Island, would be near enough for weekend visits. I couldn't wait to get started.

Yet I was sad to leave Ireland. The damp, dreary weather aside, I had been happy there. I had come to love the hilarious, profane chatter in Irish pubs; nights out at the theater; my long strolls down Grafton Street; and the quiet reflection afforded by my cathedral visits. My professors had treated me with respect, my classmates regarded me as an equal, and the Farrars had become my second family. Ruth and Ivan's kids were teenagers by then, and in many ways, I had grown up with them. The Farrars had surrounded me with warmth and friendship and kept me on an even keel as I worked through the pressures of medical school and the emotional upheaval of leaving home and being in a strange country. They never failed to ask me how my day went, were genuinely interested in hearing my descriptions of various medical processes, and shared in the joy of my accomplishments. I would miss them terribly. But I had my destiny to fulfill, and I had to go for it.

I gave the Fiat 500 to Ruth, packed my bags, took the Farrars out for a final dinner together, and said my farewells.

It was summer 1975, and I was on the move again, headed for another foreign country, ready to take on the next challenge. I had only a student visa good for one year, but I wasn't nervous. I was thirty-three years old, not a kid anymore. I knew who I was and what I wanted, and I believed to my core that I had the grit to make it. I was Dr. Himmet Dajee, the boy named Courage, and I was on top of the world.

nine

ONWARD TO CANADA

MY LIVING SITUATION IN HALIFAX was quite different from my homey lodgings in Ireland. Because I was committed for just one year, I had arranged to board in the apartments reserved for interns that were located in a veterans hospital where I'd be doing some of my training. It was little more than a glorified dorm room, but what it lacked in charm it more than made up for by being rent-free and extremely convenient. I was going to be very busy, and I only needed a place to lay my head.

I quickly learned that frigid Canada was different from soggy Ireland in many ways, but I came to love the lifestyle and the people just as much. Like the Irish, the Canadians I met were almost always friendly. But they were more open-minded, less traditional, and they possessed a hardy streak no doubt bred into them by surviving long, harsh winters; a rugged, rocky landscape; and a maritime history as salty as they come.

Halifax is a unique and wonderful place. The capital of Nova Scotia, it lies about 550 miles northeast of Portland, Maine, on a large peninsula which, if viewed from above the earth, would seem to hang like a partially severed appendage trying mightily to cling to the mainland and avoid being swept off into the icy North Atlantic Ocean. It was founded in the mid-eighteenth century by Edward Cornwallis, a British aristocrat and military man who was uncle to Lord Charles Cornwallis, the general who famously surrendered at Yorktown, bringing the American Revolution to a close. Originally a military stronghold prized for its strategic position and large natural harbor, it became in the nineteenth and early twentieth centuries the Canadian equivalent of Ellis Island—the main entry point for European immigrants, mostly of English, Scottish, and Irish stock. In the 1970s, the city was known for its busy seaport and picturesque waterfront, although it wasn't yet the tourist destination it later became thanks to its designation as a stopping point for many cruise ships.

One of the first things I noticed about Halifax was that locals never got the memo about Canada being an independent country, as the city seemed very much still a part of the British Empire. Almost everything of note in the city was named after Queen Victoria or Queen Elizabeth. *Come on, what century are we living in?* I thought during my initial inspection. Aside from the waterfront area, the city was dominated by the Citadel, a naval base turned historic site overlooking the harbor on Halifax's highest hill, where kilt-wearing Highlanders stand guard to this day.

Although I threw myself into my work as an intern, I used whatever free time I had to see the sights and learn the local customs. The fall in Halifax was unbelievable, like nothing I'd ever seen before. From September to November, the leaves all changed color as if a painter with a palette of fiery red, gold, and orange had swept a brush across the landscape. I went to see maple trees tapped to extract the sweet sap and saw maple candies being made. I'd go for walks along the waterfront, stopping in at the seafood restaurants and bars fronting the harbor. In the winter, I was surprised by the soft silence of the snow, how it would drift down with a whisper and muffle the sounds of the city.

I learned about the annual ritual of putting on snow tires every November and removing them six months later, which was quite astonishing for a guy who grew up in Africa. I quickly came to appreciate the importance of a well-made boot, and I was careful to heed the locals' warnings not to walk under the eaves of buildings in the springtime, to avoid being pierced by falling icicles. When I first heard the sound of ice cracking on a river, I was startled. It was as if a huge carpet of glass was shattering. The Bay of Fundy, which borders Nova Scotia to the west, was a natural wonder that I loved to visit. Its extraordinary tides, fueled by sixty billion tons of seawater flowing in and out during each cycle, could reach an astonishing five stories.

My first year in Halifax was a whirlwind of one-month rotations at local hospitals—Victoria General, Halifax Infirmary, and Izaak Walton Killam Hospital for Children. I rotated through general medicine, pediatric medicine, general surgery a few times, urology, thoracic surgery, vascular surgery, obstetrics and gynecology, and cardiology. I went on rounds with residents, took patient histories, drew blood, ordered tests, made diagnoses, and suggested courses of treatment, as I had done in Ireland, with one important difference: just as I had seen at the Mayo Clinic, there was less emphasis on examining and talking to patients and more on lab work and other tests. This concerned me, because the Royal College had taught me to listen to and observe patients carefully as the best way to come to an accurate diagnosis. Tests are run, but they are used largely as a means of confirming a diagnosis, not as a fishing expedition. My old mentor, Dr. Browne, would tell us again and again, "If all else fails, examine the patient." It's hard to believe, but that's a step that many doctors, particularly those trained in North America, routinely miss.

One day well into my internship, I received a message that the dean of the entire medical school, the head guy, wanted to see me. I immediately suspected what the meeting was about, and I panicked. When I had gone through my urology rotation, I was disappointed with the way it was run. I found the department disorganized; everything was done in a rush. I felt that this increased the odds of errors being made. At the end of each rotation, we were asked to review our experiences, and I was brutally honest about my observations of urology. I wrote a critique of the department and included a ten-point plan for improvement. But as I trudged to the dean's office, I realized that I had gone too far. I would be seen as a brash upstart, and

I would be asked to leave. My student visa wouldn't be renewed. It would be the end of my short career in Canada, and I'd be forced to return shamefaced to South Africa.

I sat before the dean's desk, barely able to conceal my terror. My assessment was lying in front of him, and he was gazing down at it. Then he looked up at me and said that he had asked to see me because he wanted to thank me. "I wish we had more physicians like you," he said. "We really appreciate your comments." It was all I could do to keep from falling out of my chair.

Not long after that, I was preparing to be interviewed by the director of Dalhousie's residency program regarding my application for a general surgical residency. Again, I had reason to be nervous. So much was riding on this moment. I had taken a chance on coming to Canada with only a one-year commitment. Now my whole future career depended on getting accepted into a surgical residency program. But as I waited to be called in for my interview, the director's secretary whispered to me, "I think you're in." Flushed with confidence, I relaxed and breezed through the interview. Sure enough, I was offered a spot. A few days later, I received another acceptance from McMaster University, just outside Toronto. I thought about it briefly, but I was happy at Dalhousie, so I decided to stay on for the next four years as a surgical resident.

I bought a used Chevy Monza for $2,000 and began looking for an apartment. I was ready to settle in.

The apartment I rented when I finished my internship was just what I had been looking for. It was in a building in a university-owned complex, where I would enjoy an unobstructed view of the scenic harbor, underground parking, and proximity to the many other medical and surgical residents who lived there. Best of all, it was just a short walk to the hospital where I'd be doing some of my surgical training.

But for the first three months of my residency, I was sent, along with three other first-year residents, to St. John Regional

Hospital, a small community teaching hospital located across the Bay of Fundy in New Brunswick. There I did my first general surgical rotation and boarded in the hospital's spartan living quarters—basically a room with a bed. But that first rotation was an amazing experience, because some excellent surgeons oversaw my training, and I was allowed to take on more responsibilities, such as teaching interns and performing a larger volume of surgical work than I had previously. I worked as hard as ever trying to make a favorable impression.

We residents were routinely asked to prepare presentations on such topics as complications of bowel surgery or how to manage appendicitis. We had to know anatomy backward and forward, the layers a surgeon must go through to reach the abdominal organs, and where to look for an appendix that might be in an abnormal position. Knowledge of physiological function was equally important, for surgeons aren't merely technicians but must also carefully monitor kidneys, lungs, and many other organs and be able to interpret all the data from various tests and monitors. What's more, we had to prepare patients for surgery and answer question after question our teachers sprung on us. Where do you make the incision? What if you open a belly and can't find what you're looking for? What do you do? What steps should you take if the patient's condition deteriorates while you are operating? We reviewed methodology and were reminded that we must always return all the organs that we explored to their original positions. It was fascinating work.

I had no complaints about my social life either. I would go to movies, restaurants, and parties with the three other residents who were doing the rotation with me, and there was no shortage of pretty women to meet. During my stay in New Brunswick, I dated a charming nurse who took me to her parents' home for dinner, where we ate the most humungous lobsters I'd ever seen. I hadn't been in Canada long before I learned that the women there were far more liberal and free-spirited than the ones I'd met in Ireland. Religion was always a powerful presence in Ireland, but even if that didn't prove to be an obstacle and a young woman was willing, intimate relationships could still be a tricky business, because the country had banned the sale of condoms and other contraceptive devices. In Canada, I was still a long way from settling down, but I certainly wasn't going to deprive myself of the very agreeable female companionship that was abundantly available during my long residency there.

Busy as I was, I still made it a point to keep up with the news back home, and I exchanged letters with my siblings as often as possible. For South Africans, 1976 was shaping up to be a pivotal year. The rest of the world was finally waking up to the brutal injustice of the apartheid regime. At the Summer Olympics, which were held in Montreal that year, thirty-two African nations staged a walkout over the International Olympic Committee's refusal to ban New Zealand because its national rugby team was touring South Africa. And a student-led movement to pressure universities and businesses to divest their stocks and other holdings connected to South Africa was beginning to mobilize on U.S. campuses. Everywhere I went, people quizzed me about life in South Africa. They were hungry to know just how bad it really was.

On June 16 of that year, right about the time I was completing my Canadian internship, a tragic but seminal event in the history of South Africa began when students in the Soweto township outside Johannesburg joined in what started as a peaceful protest march. The seeds of the trouble had been sown back in 1953, when the government had passed the Bantu Education Act, a blatantly racist law that laid out a system of apartheid in the country's schools.

Prior to the act, most schools attended by black children were run by missionaries with some state aid. But under the new system, government funding was made conditional on the acceptance of a racially discriminatory curriculum administered by the new Department of Bantu Education, and even then, the funds allocated were just a fraction of those spent on education for whites. It guaranteed that black children would be packed into dilapidated schoolrooms where there was little money to spend even on the most basic essentials, such as textbooks and well-trained teachers. Much as I had hated my life in South Africa, at least I'd received a decent education. The black population didn't even have that. After all, why would the Afrikaners want blacks to be educated when they intended to keep them subjugated as menial laborers?

But the government wasn't done screwing over the blacks yet. In 1976, a decree was issued that imposed the Afrikaans language as the medium of instruction in all public middle schools and high schools. Not only was Afrikaans the hated language of the oppressors but most blacks weren't fluent in it, so making it the compulsory language in schools would have put any meaningful learning even further out of reach. On that morning in June, thousands of students gathered in Soweto to sing songs and march toward the Orlando soccer stadium where a peaceful rally to protest the new decree had been planned. They never made it to the stadium. On the way, they were met by police officers, who tried to stop the march with tear gas and warning shots. Then the police began firing directly into the crowd, and the South African security forces poured into Soweto with armored tanks and live ammunition. Police dogs were let loose on the protestors. By the end of the day, hundreds of people—many only children—were killed or injured. The photo of a fellow student carrying the mortally wounded twelve-year-old Hector Pieterson was published around the world, igniting international outrage.

Over the following months, the Soweto Uprising grew into a national protest movement, and chaos and violence broke out in cities all over the country. Reports spread of protestors taken to jail and tortured. The death toll mounted; by some estimates, more than a thousand were killed.

I monitored these reports with increasing alarm, and both Amrit and I continued urging our siblings to leave South Africa as soon as possible. Dhiraj and his family were settled in Johannesburg by that time and remained unwilling to consider moving abroad. But Bhanu and Anjuli, along with my sisters Padma and Hansa, seemed increasingly open to the idea, and we wrote many letters back and forth, and talked by telephone about it. Yet they continued to hesitate.

Fortunately, Padma and Hansa had been out of the country when the worst of the violence swept through South Africa, so at least I knew they were out of harm's way. They had arranged to visit the United States for the first time and had spent the summer traveling coast to coast. It was a wonderful time to visit, for it was the American Bicentennial, and all over the nation, the ideals of freedom and democracy were being celebrated. I had hoped that Bhanu and Anjuli would come too, but Bhanu had said he was too tied up his in business dealings to leave. I hoped that at least my sisters' long visit might encourage them finally to decide to seek a better life in the United States. Amrit—by then a U.S. citizen—had been looking into the legal immigration process on their behalf.

By early September, the girls were back with Amrit, who was just completing his cardiothoracic surgical residency at Brown University in Rhode Island. They planned to continue on to visit South America, but before they left, I was to fly down to Providence to meet them.

ten

THAT CURSED COUNTRY

AS MY RENDEZVOUS WITH AMRIT, Padma, and Hansa grew closer, I continued my work at St. John in New Brunswick. I was so preoccupied with my training, and with enjoying my new surroundings, that I barely had time to think about anything else, including the upcoming reunion with my sisters. My thoughts were focused entirely on surgery, and, quite frankly, I was having a good time.

Consumed as I was with work and socializing, it never occurred to me to think it a bit odd when, one day at the hospital, I was told that I had a call from my brother. I didn't even give it a second thought. Amrit and I spoke on the phone frequently, although we usually called each other after our normal working hours. It didn't register with me that it was unusual for him to be calling when he must have known that I was immersed in my duties at the hospital. Nor did I immediately recognize the very particular tone he used when he began to speak, or the careful manner in which he chose his words.

Throughout the many long years of training and the myriad details, processes, and procedures that a surgeon must master, we must all learn to grapple with one inevitable part of the job: delivering the worst news to a patient's loved ones. Some surgeons I've known have never felt equipped to deal with this grim task. One senior surgeon under whom I trained became so unglued by the prospect that he always sent the junior guys like me to speak to the family. I soon realized that the gentlest, most humane way to tell a family that they had lost a loved one was to ease into it. I would review the patient's medical issues, starting with something like "As you know, John was suffering from . . ." And then I would go on to explain all the steps that we had taken to try to save him. Finally, as the realization of where I was going with all this began to sink in with the family, I would say how sorry I was that nothing more could have been done and that the patient was gone.

I didn't immediately pick up on that same slow, patient style of speaking Amrit was using to tell me why he was calling that day. "As you know," he began, "there's been a lot of violence going on back home." The Soweto Uprising had spread to Cape Town, he reminded me, and the police had responded with ferocity to shut down the protests. Some of those demonstrations had been taking place in the streets of Retreat, the colored township where Bhanu's store was located.

I didn't see it coming. For all the hatred I held in my heart for apartheid, and despite my unshakable belief that nothing good could ever happen in that cursed country, I always thought that if I just kept moving, South Africa couldn't hurt me anymore. But I was so very wrong. For what Amrit was so delicately trying to tell me on that awful day in September 1976 was that my beloved brother Bhanu was dead. He had been gunned down like a dog on the streets of Cape Town.

Shock. Disbelief. Trying not to collapse. *This can't be true,* I thought. "Is this true?" I whispered. Amrit assured me that it was, yet I couldn't take it in, couldn't accept what he was saying. *No,* I thought. *Just no.* Not Bhanu. Anyone but Bhanu, the most caring, generous man I'd ever known, the guy everyone loved, the brother who would sooner cut off his own arm than hurt another. Not him. It's just not possible that he could die in such a way. It just couldn't be.

Bits and pieces of what happened next come back to me in a haze of dreadful memories that I've tried to block out over the years. I know that Amrit told me that he had received the news from Dhiraj's wife, Belle. Anjuli was in pieces. We had to fly home immediately. They were delaying the funeral to give Amrit, Padma, Hansa, and me time to get there. I would meet the others, and we would travel to South Africa together. I vaguely recall walking numbly down the hall to see the chairman of the Department of Surgery at St. John to ask for time off. I went home and quickly packed.

Within a day, the four of us were on a flight to London, where we would change planes before continuing on with our long, excruciating journey back to Cape Town. The flying time alone took a full day. I quietly wept the entire way.

A somber crowd of about two dozen family members and friends met us at the airport.

Through the tears, some of the details surrounding Bhanu's killing were sketched out for us, while other facts I learned years later.

The Soweto Uprising had spread throughout all corners of South Africa, and on September 8, mobs of angry demonstrators surged through the streets of Cape Town, turning the city into a war zone. Bhanu and Anjuli were terrified. The situation was so bad that they had decided to stock up on groceries and other staples in case they were forced to hunker down in their house in Rylands Estates. But, despite their fears, Bhanu decided that they should both leave home that morning. First, he went to speak to our father, to try to convince him to keep his shop on Sir Lowry Road closed. He talked to our half brother Naresh as well, beseeching him to take care and avoid going out. And then, although he knew that some of the worst of the rioting was occurring in Retreat, where his business was located, Bhanu decided to go there anyway.

It was a fateful decision. I can't explain why he made that choice, but I suppose I shouldn't have been surprised that he was thinking of everyone else's welfare before his own.

After Bhanu and Anjuli arrived at their shop, the surrounding streets were overrun by the angry mob. Demonstrators poured down the road singing liberation songs, while others took the opportunity to raise havoc, smashing windows and looting stores. Heavily armed police squads moved in to quash the unrest. For some time, Bhanu and Anjuli hid in the toilet in the back of their shop, but after a while, they fled to a building across the street, where their friends had stores with living quarters above. They remained upstairs there for some time, shaking and crying, realizing that any chance they might have had to flee the area was long gone. There was no way they could drive through the melee. On the street below, police were tossing protestors, some only children, into their vehicles.

But Bhanu was worried because he had left a set of keys to his shop in his car. When the situation on the street had quieted somewhat, he made another fatal decision. He decided to retrieve the keys. Four or five of the other shop owners agreed to accompany him. As they crossed the threshold onto the street, they saw a gathering of armed police and shouted to them not to shoot, that they were only shop owners.

The police opened fire anyway. Everyone in the group was hit by buckshot pellets. One guy was hit in the arm, another in the leg. But it was Bhanu who took the brunt of the barrage. He collapsed to the ground. Anjuli, still in the apartment upstairs, rushed down to the street, where she cradled her blood-soaked husband and shouted for an ambulance. He was warm to the touch, and at first she thought that if they could get him to a hospital quickly, he could be saved. Then she was belted with the horrific reality of their circumstances: an ambulance or medical workers could never get to them in time. Bhanu, riddled with fifty or sixty buckshot pellets to the chest, was doomed. He died on the dirty pavement as Anjuli held him in her arms.

More people were gathered at Bhanu's house when we arrived. Because the Hindu tradition is to hold funeral services within a day after death, and the family had already delayed for Amrit, Padma, Hansa, and me, everyone responded with haste once we were there. Amrit had decided to go to the morgue to identify and claim the body, and he asked me to accompany him. "No," I told him, "you go. I just can't bear it." The truth was simple: I lacked the courage. But it wasn't long before the coffin arrived at the house, and it was opened for a brief time for us to pay our respects.

There he lay. Only his face, puffy and distorted, was visible. My mind flashed back to the boy I had watched die back in Ireland, and I hoped that my brother hadn't lingered too long in agony.

I can't claim that my choice of professions had made me completely inured to death, but I had by then acquired a certain understanding and acceptance of it. Sometimes things go wrong in the body, and nothing we physicians can do will prevent the inevitable. All we can do is give those in our care some peace at the end.

This was different. It was a monstrous, deliberate snuffing out of a vibrant, extraordinary life. I felt a sharp, savage pain that I had never before known—not even when my mother had died. Bhanu had been just thirty-seven years old, and he was a decent and gracious man, with everything to live for. He would have been a huge success if he had just left South Africa. My God, he was so ambitious! With his entrepreneurial instincts, he could have gone far if he had made it to North America. All he'd needed was a ticket, just to get on a plane and get the hell out of that toxic place. As I gazed at my brother for the last time, the pain began to turn to anger, and the anger into pure, searing rage.

The service at the crematorium was surreal. There was the usual chanting and reciting of passages in Hindi and Sanskrit; the familiar scent of burning incense, sandalwood, and ghee; and much weeping. People gave speeches. Just as it was at my mother's funeral, everything at the ceremony merged into an incomprehensible drone in my head. But unlike at my mother's funeral, there was no open pyre. Instead, a door opened, and the casket was sent through to the flames beyond. I suppose it was meant to be more civilized and modern, but to me it felt too austere and sanitized. I had no affinity for the Hindu religion, but I yearned for a speck of comfort from imagining Bhanu's beautiful spirit rising into the sky far above the troubles and terrors of the world.

Back at the house, the customary vegetarian dishes made with eggplant, okra, lentils, and peas were served with roti, and glasses of whiskey and brandy were raised in memory of Bhanu and to wish him well on his journey to a higher plane. Some people reminisced, while others continued to weep. Anjuli and my sisters were just broken.

My father was devastated. Sons aren't supposed to die before their parents, and he seemed unable to take it in. But my compassion was checked when he continued to question why Bhanu had decided to set up his business in Retreat. "He should never have been there," he kept repeating, as if Bhanu had somehow been responsible for his own death. I set aside a piece of my fury at South Africa and directed it toward my father.

There was no apology. No investigation. No one was ever held responsible for Bhanu's killing. The World Council of Churches at one point offered to look into it, but we didn't follow up. I realize how difficult that might be for others to understand. Of course we wanted answers and accountability. Who fired the shots? Did someone give an order to shoot, and if so, why? Was Bhanu targeted intentionally, or was it a grotesque mistake? Did my brother's death merely amount to just another case of cold-blooded indifference on the part of police, who saw dark skin and reflexively opened fire, even as Bhanu and his friends shouted at them not to shoot?

The questions tormented us. But this was South Africa. It was my utter belief that justice did not and never would exist there. The police lied as a matter of routine, and they were part of a system that was so entrenched, so powerful, that any effort to uncover the facts would only end in more pain and tears.

Besides, I knew what killed Bhanu. The bloody Afrikaners killed him. Apartheid killed him.

South Africa killed him.

I hadn't thought it was possible to hate my native country any more than I already did, but I was wrong about that too. I saw no point in lingering too long after the funeral. Padma and Hansa stayed behind; they had decided to continue living with Anjuli for the time being. Amrit headed back to the United States by way of Ireland, where he spent a few days visiting with the Farrars. Many years later, I learned that he had unloaded on Ruth his crushing grief over Bhanu's death. As for me, I flew back to Canada with only my rage to keep me company. And I made another vow to myself.

I would never set foot in South Africa again.

A light had gone out. The world without Bhanu was a dimmer place. Yet even as I despaired that Bhanu would never get a chance to pursue his dreams, I also knew that he wouldn't want me to give up on mine. As I returned to work in Canada, I reminded myself of the promise I'd made when I first left South Africa. I would not look back. I would wipe all the heartache and anger from my memory, or at least bury it so deeply that it would have no power over me and couldn't hinder me from achieving my goals.

But a few days after my return, the past reached out a pitiless hand to yank me back.

I went to check my mail. I saw the familiar blue airmail envelope that told me that someone had written from overseas. Nothing unusual about that. Then I saw the writing on the outside and my heart nearly stopped: it was Bhanu's.

I ripped the letter open and read it, then reread it, hardly able to believe what was happening. It was as if my brother were communicating with me across some great void. He was dead, yet here he was. And he had something important to tell me.

I'm coming, he wrote. At long last, Bhanu was leaving South Africa, and he would join me in my new world.

The letter was dated September 3, 1976, five days before his death.

Callous, mocking fate. I called Amrit and read the letter to him. He couldn't believe it either. We talked for a while, but there was nothing more to say or do. It was as if I'd had a knife driven through my heart, and now it was being twisted this way and that by the tragic irony of Bhanu's final wishes. The last time I had seen him alive, after my medical school graduation, he had seemed uncharacteristically discouraged. But with his decision to settle his affairs in South Africa and try his luck abroad, perhaps he'd had reason to hope for the first time in years.

Yet his letter also revealed his worries and fears—about the increasing violence taking over the city, the difficulties he would encounter trying to sell his business, and what kind of prospects he would have in the United States. His anguished state of mind was evident in the rushed manner and broken language in which his letter was written.

> Dear Himmet,
>
> I am surprised no reply to my letter to date. Have I mentioned anything wrong that may have been offensive or are you occupied and unable to reply soon. I take it that you have discussed my letter on your trip to Providence.

Letter? What letter? I've wracked my brain, but I still can't recall. Could I have been so engrossed in my work that I had overlooked his previous attempt to communicate with me about something so important?

> I am sorry to rush, as I am anxious to know what has transpired—decisions taken. Since I've to plan accordingly. All I want is the girls to be over until I get there—a family get together on foreign soil and so we can discuss and settle problems of mutual interest— 'blueprint.' Don't worry the responsibility of the girls is and will remain mine—if that is the fear.

This was all so characteristic of Bhanu. His need for a plan, and his assurances that he would continue to care for our sisters. He was always thinking of others. But it was clear that he still worried greatly about his prospects if he moved to the United States. Amrit and I had certainly been prepared to help him find a suitable situation, and as a U.S. citizen, Amrit was in a position to sponsor him. But at the time, neither of us was making a great deal of money, and neither of us knew where we would eventually settle. And Bhanu had the added complications of trying to sell his house and extricate himself from his business, neither of which would have been easy given the unstable climate in South Africa. Those were the thoughts that weighed on Bhanu in his final days, yet he'd made it clear that he had finally committed to a course of action.

> I am now prepared to settle abroad—but where, this is what I intend to discuss when I am on the scene with all present. Isn't it proper than think wishfully from here. Don't forget it's not easy for me to uproot. I have to dispose of my assets etc. Then I have to find something suitable to do—earn a living with my education and maintain the same living standards I enjoyed here.
>
> In times like we have here now there are no buyers for the shop or house—the market is flat. Did you see or read in newspaper what's going on. Riots gone crazy every day, one can't get into town if you drive through nonwhite areas you get stoned, smash your car up—dangerous or get shot, yes in Cape Town unheard of. All high school students are disrupting services etc., the schools are closed for a week—don't know what's happening next. Business is bad. Thank god the girls are not here, they would not have gone to work as you must go to work past Klipfontain Road, and can't move freely. Yet they want to get back. I haven't written to them about this episode—it started a week ago.
>
> Good that I did not come over it would have upset me to hear from afar if you haven't seen what it [*sic*] like. I will definitely be able to come over after

97

January?? Having taken school business I will be at
ease. Hoping that the situation changes here. Should
business become very very bad at least all my liabilities
are covered, at least I'll be and feel free for a year.
Everyone is now thinking in terms of preparing for the
day to come should it get bad.

Best of luck,
Bhanu

I've reread and reanalyzed the letter a thousand times over
the years, and through every job change and every move I've
made, I've held on to it. Historians now say the Soweto Uprising
was a major turning point in the struggle against apartheid, the
event that spurred worldwide condemnation of the South African
government and pressure for it to liberalize. Even though many
more years passed and many more lives were lost before change
finally came to South Africa, Bhanu's blood was part of that
history, his letter a testament to the toll that oppression can take
on humanity. Of course, back then, I still firmly believed that
conditions in South Africa would only get worse, never better.
For me, keeping the letter was a way to hold on to a small piece
of my brother, though only his hauntingly tragic final words to
me. It brought me no peace, yet it was all I had left of him.

But then something happened right after I returned to Canada,
which was in a way a last gift to me from Bhanu. While I had
been away in South Africa for the funeral, the dean and the
chairman of the Department of Surgery had together written to
the government ministry in charge of immigration on my behalf.
A few days after my return, I learned that I had been granted
refugee status on the grounds that my brother had been shot as
a result of the political turmoil in South Africa. The change in
my designation gave me an added measure of security, because
I had previously held only a temporary student visa that had to
be renewed annually. It was Canada's way of showing me that
I was welcome to stay.

Even in death, Bhanu was looking out for me.

eleven

CARRYING ON

I COULD SO EASILY HAVE SUCCUMBED to my anger and resentment and spiraled into depression, the kind of self-defeating mental state that Bhanu had always helped me keep at bay. Perhaps I might have soldiered on, but in a beaten-down, halfhearted fashion, knowing that the loss of the person I'd loved more than any other was the final blow that had broken me. South Africa would have won at last.

But for as long as I could remember, I had been cultivating my emotional survival skills, and I had put those skills to good use in the tightrope existence of a surgeon in training. No matter how stressful the situation, or how angry or torn up I felt inside, I had learned always to maintain a calm exterior. I might be pushed to the brink of my abilities, quite literally holding someone's life in my hands, but that unruffled facade would never crumble. It wasn't heartlessness, although some people might have thought me a bit chilly or detached. I see it more as being able to compartmentalize. I can keep my anxieties, heartaches, disappointments, and anger locked away and focus instead on what needs to be done. This is what allowed me to keep my hands steady while performing open-heart surgery later in my career, and it's how I was able to move forward without letting my grief over Bhanu's death destroy me.

When I returned to Canada to resume my surgical training after the worst tragedy I'd ever experienced, I recognized that I had a choice. I could either let my anguish overwhelm me, or I could immerse myself in work. I chose work. Indeed, I became more relentlessly determined, more intensely focused on my career than ever before. I had embarked on a journey to accomplish something, and by God, nothing was going to stop me now. I would not, could not, ever forget Bhanu. He would live on inside me, in my thoughts and in the very blood that coursed through my veins, every moment of every day for the rest of my life. Yet my patients would know nothing of this interior life of mine. I would hold my love for my brother, along with my poisonous hatred for the country that killed him, in a place deep inside that others couldn't reach. That was how I would carry on.

And so in October, just a month after the funeral, I traveled back to London for the final set of exams I needed to pass to earn my second medical degree. I passed, and my new diploma was awarded the following month. It might seem curious—odd even—that at this point, I still thought it so important to expend the extra effort to get that degree, since I was already well on my way to becoming a surgeon. But it made perfect sense to me to finish what I'd started. The British medical system was revered throughout the world, and having a University of London degree would be a way to distinguish myself throughout my career.

I felt certain that Bhanu would have been proud.

Back in Halifax, I threw myself into my work with a singular ferocity. Bhanu was gone, but I could still heal others, so that was what I was going to do. As I continued with my first-year residency rotations, I made it a point to look for other ways to push myself and add to my credentials. One way to do this was to become involved in research, which meant engaging in more laboratory work and writing research papers for publication in medical journals.

I had coauthored my first paper back in Dublin with an Irish cardiologist under whom I worked during my first internship.

Dr. Eoin O'Brien had suggested that we collaborate on a paper dealing with a condition known as Friedreich's ataxia, a rare inherited disorder that causes neurological damage. One of my assigned tasks was to interview an Irish family that suffered from this genetic malady. When our paper was finally published, in 1977, we were among the first in the medical community to link the disorder to cardiac disease.

Dr. O'Brien had impressed on me the importance of building a reputation by conducting research and writing papers of this kind, so I was bent on getting published at every opportunity. Fortunately, plenty of chances presented themselves in Halifax. I got my start there thanks to a cardiac surgeon named David Murphy, who was also a brilliant researcher. He ran experiments in what we colloquially referred to as his dog lab at Izaak Walton Killam Hospital for Children. Dog hearts are similar enough to human hearts to be useful for trying out new theories and techniques. My second paper, on which I collaborated during my first year of residency, involved working with Dr. Murphy on isolating the right atrium as a pump in congenital heart disease cases, as a means of restoring blood flow to the lungs. It was published in 1978 in the *Journal of Thoracic and Cardiovascular Surgery,* one of the top cardiac surgical journals.

Altogether, I cowrote six papers while I was at Dalhousie, each one another feather in my cap. One of them involved a case in which a twenty-year-old woman's abdominal aorta ruptured during a car crash. We showed that the rupture was caused by her seat belt; most seat belts in those days crossed the lap but lacked a shoulder strap. I like to think that our paper added to the growing body of evidence showing that the lap belts alone could cause serious injury.

I loved working with Dr. Murphy and the other researchers in the dog lab; they were all great thinkers. I would take every opening available to help them with various tasks, from holding instruments to assisting with dissections. The work gave me great insight into heart surgery and fueled my continuing interest in finding improved ways of doing things. We'd often sit around a table, drink coffee, and discuss ways to devise a better gizmo, and

I found this routine both comforting and energizing; it reminded me of my old brainstorming sessions with Bhanu.

One problem we puzzled over was how to stabilize a patient whose ribs were fractured due to trauma. Patients in that condition can develop what's called a flail chest—when they try to take a deep inward breath, the chest collapses and prevents the lungs from expanding. We physicians would put these patients on ventilators for several weeks while the bones healed, but this was an imperfect solution, because it could lead to a narrowing of the trachea, and infections like pneumonia could set in. In the dog lab, as we mulled over different possible means of external stabilization, such as pins, plates, or struts, I thought to myself, *This is why I went into this field. To make an impact.* And when Dr. Murphy invited me to his beautiful home, I wondered if I'd ever be as accomplished, and as highly respected, as he was.

That year, I also won a $500 surgical prize from Dalhousie for my contributions to a study in which newborn rats were injected with the bacterium that causes pneumonia. We found that an immune stimulant called levamisole protected the infected rats from dying. I submitted my work for presentation at the Royal College of Surgeons in Australia and was accepted. In 1980, toward the end of my residency, I traveled there to present the findings. The following year, I made the same presentation at the Society of University Surgeons in Hershey, Pennsylvania.

Yet another presentation had taken me in 1978 to a meeting of the Canadian Cardiovascular Society in Vancouver, where I shared the results of a study on the management of left coronary artery disease cases. In those days, intra-aortic balloon pumps were inserted prior to surgery in these high-mortality cases, but we had demonstrated that surgery could be performed safely without the balloons and the risk of additional complications they posed. My cap was bristling with feathers.

As a resident, I now had opportunities to teach as well. One incident during my first-year general surgical rotation stands out. I had visited a patient who had been suffering right upper quadrant pain, that is, pain in the area just below the right rib cage. I asked the medical student under my charge to offer a diagnosis, and he went through a whole gamut of possibilities, all of which we were able to rule out for various reasons. Finally, I asked the student to lift up the patient's gown. Sure enough, there was a blistering rash on the skin in the area where the patient had reported experiencing pain. It was a textbook case of shingles. Once again, I could hear my old mentor, Dr. Browne, saying, "If all else fails, examine the patient."

Another case I'll never forget involved a patient who had worked on the railway. He had fallen while trying to link two cars together, and both of his legs were crushed under the wheels. By the time I saw him, he was in hemorrhagic shock. I was stunned by his condition. I'd never seen someone so white. All I could do was give him fluids, blood, and pain medication and call for an orthopedic surgeon. He lost both legs, but he survived.

Not everything I did won me plaudits. I recall in particular a case during that first year involving a boy of about nine who had undergone surgery to remove a tumor from his adrenal gland. Sadly, he died a few days later. The senior doctor on the case gathered the team to talk it over and asked us for thoughts about why the patient had succumbed. I suggested that it could have been a pulmonary embolism, which is a blockage in one of the arteries in the lungs, a condition usually caused by blood clots, but one that is rare in children. The doctor in charge shot me down, criticizing me harshly in front of my peers and stating in a condescending way that it couldn't possibly be a pulmonary embolism in someone so young. I was mortified and felt myself shrink before my colleagues' eyes as I fought to keep my old insecurities at bay. Later an autopsy identified the cause of death: pulmonary embolism. I never got an apology or an acknowledgment that I'd been right, but I didn't care about that. I knew I'd been vindicated.

Even though I was just a first-year resident, I got a lot of experience performing surgeries—appendectomies, splenectomies, hernia repairs, you name it. I learned to think fast on my feet and make ample use of that aura of calm confidence that I had so carefully cultivated. Once during a middle-of-the-night operation to remove an inflamed gallbladder, the senior surgeon on the case arrived late, obviously intoxicated. I always knew when this guy was drunk because he chewed on mints in a transparent attempt to mask the smell of alcohol. He was only meant to oversee me as I performed the surgery, and to assist me as needed, so I thought that despite his condition, I had the situation under control. I gave him a simple task—to hold a clamp and gently pull the gallbladder aside, to make room for me to dissect the cystic artery and cystic duct and suture the areas from which they had been removed. But suddenly he jerked, pulling on the clamp so hard that he yanked the entire gallbladder out. It was a mistake fraught with danger, for if the artery started to bleed or if bile leaked into the abdominal cavity, we would be in big trouble. I had to react quickly and, above all, not panic. Fortunately, the artery was so inflamed that it didn't bleed, and I sutured it closed.

I was going to take the bloody thing out anyway, but for a first-year resident, it was a difficult surgery. We were lucky that the patient ultimately recovered and that he never knew what had happened while he slept away under anesthesia. My inebriated colleague, looking particularly sheepish, merely said, "Sorry, Himmet."

In 1977, Canada did me another favor. I was granted landed immigrant status, replacing the refugee status I'd held since my return from Bhanu's funeral in 1976. It was a great relief, as I'd always had a niggling fear in the back of my mind that somehow things could still go awry and I'd be forced to return to South Africa. This new designation meant that I had been accepted as a permanent resident and could stay as long as I wanted. It was also another indication of the kindness, compassion, and inclusiveness of the Canadian people, whom I had come to admire greatly.

I was working pretty much seven days a week, and I was so busy I'd eat both breakfast and lunch at the hospital, but for dinner, I usually had the luxury of either going out to eat or cooking for myself. Faculty members frequently invited me to dinners and parties, and I was often included in celebrations around Christmas and New Year. But since I was living alone and not with a family like the Farrars, these affairs were more like professional get-togethers. Generally speaking, though, I found the Canadians to be far less formal and tradition bound, and definitely less religious, than the Irish. Work hard and play hard—that was the motto in Canada.

There were lots of lovely women to date, and I often found myself accompanying nurses to parties. They were the best partiers; they really knew how to let their hair down. Once while we were scrubbing up before an operation, two nurses grabbed hold of me and dumped me in a tub filled with hot water. My clothes, as well as my trusty beeper, were soaked. So I did the first thing that came to mind: I retaliated, managing to get hold of one of my tormentors, wrangle her into another tub, and turn all three faucets on full blast. We roared with laughter, but I shudder now to think how such practical joking would be viewed today.

I learned a tremendous lot from the nurses with whom I worked. They were on the front lines, interacting with the patients, helping manage their care and dealing with the families. They understood procedure and protocol, but they also showed me how to inject a welcome degree of humanity into clinical proceedings. They held the hands of parents who had lost their children, guiding them through the traumatic aftermath with helpful information about funeral homes and other details. Anybody with a brain can learn how to operate. But to communicate with families under the most trying circumstances—that, to me, is truly heroic. It's no wonder those same nurses sometimes needed to blow off steam.

But the nurses were by no means the only ones who knew how to cut loose. Once a year was held an eagerly anticipated golf tournament, in which the residents took on the faculty. Everyone would load his or her golf bag with beer and liquor, and by the eighteenth hole, nobody could remember what the score was. There was a big discussion at the end of the day about who had won, but we were all so drunk that no one could figure it out, and frankly, no one cared. I think the solution was to grant the trophy to one side one year, and the other side the next year. I thought it was the greatest thing ever.

I had noticed that among the various specialties were distinct personality types. Many of the orthopedic surgeons, for instance, were gregarious jocks. But one orthopod under whom I worked didn't fit that mold. He was a serious, buttoned-up gentleman who had trained at Oxford University and who had taken note of my work and offered to help get me into Oxford for a one-year surgical fellowship. He assured me that I would qualify and urged me to apply, saying he'd use his influence to secure a position for me. It was a great compliment, and a difficult offer to pass up. What could be more prestigious than Oxford? But I hesitated. Even though my confidence as a surgeon was quite solid by then, I still had doubts about whether I'd measure up in such elite surroundings. Besides, I was doing well where I was, and didn't want to screw it up by compromising the continuity of my training at Dalhousie. So I said no. Now I wonder: what if I'd taken him up on his offer? It's a road not taken that has nagged me ever since.

Nonetheless, I have no regrets about continuing on with the excellent training that Dalhousie provided. As I rotated through one specialty after another, I was exposed to some top-notch physicians and surgeons, and I received a first-class education. And as my years in Halifax accumulated, my self-assurance and skill as a surgeon grew alongside, giving me a much bolder sense of authority as a professional. I displayed that authority in the operating room one day during my final year of residency. The chief of thoracic surgery was assisting me, but he kept distracting me, because his hands were constantly moving around at a time when I needed everything in the surgical field to be still and calm. At one point, I accidentally pricked one of his roving hands with a needle, and he blew up at me. This time, I didn't just shut up and take it. I told him in no uncertain terms that it was his fault and that he needed to keep his hands to himself. Afterward, the nurses who had assisted in the surgery told me they were impressed. "Nobody has the guts to challenge this guy," they said. It was a small moment, but one of the most satisfying of my career at that time.

By my third year as a resident, I needed to think about what would come next. I had determined early on that I didn't want to be a general surgeon, because that would mean working primarily with organs in the belly, which didn't particularly interest me. I am reminded of an intern who worked under me during one of my general surgical rotations. He was clutching a bunch of gloves, and when I asked him why he had so many, he told me that he was preparing for "rectal rounds." I laughed at his irreverent terminology, but these obligatory examinations were one reason general surgery held no appeal for me.

Pediatric surgery wasn't on the table either, because I didn't think I could handle operating on children all the time. That takes a special kind of fortitude that I didn't possess. I found vascular surgery intriguing, and I briefly flirted with the idea of going into plastic surgery. During my plastics rotation, I had been amazed at the intricate work I had seen performed with burn victims and survivors of breast cancer. Some of those surgeons were like artists, and I was greatly impressed with their skill and precision. I even went so far as to apply to a plastic surgery program, but I came in second to another resident, who got the spot.

At that point, I had a talk with myself. *Come on, Himmet, quit monkeying around. You know what you want, what you've always wanted.*

So along about my third year as a resident, I started applying for a cardiothoracic surgical residency. I wanted badly to be accepted into a program in the United States, my long-planned destination, in large part because that was where the action was when it came to heart surgery. It was an ambitious move, for the air was quite rarified at that level. Most schools accepted just two cardiothoracic surgical residents a year, some just one. Dalhousie didn't even have an accredited cardiac program, so I had to look elsewhere, and I had to assume that someone who was already working as a resident at the other institutions to which I applied would have a leg up. It also meant two more years of intense training. I would be nearly forty years old by the time I finished.

But I was drawn to heart surgery like nothing else, and so nothing else would do. Working on hearts seemed to me an almost sacred occupation. When I saw a chest opened to reveal the pericardial sac, and in it a beating heart, it felt pristine, almost spiritual, as if the heart were the center of its own mysterious universe. Everything begins and ends with the heart: the blood entering one way and exiting another, round and round in a circle that continuously replenishes the body. On a more elemental level, fixing hearts meant saving lives, and I was dead certain that that was what I was meant to do.

It was an exciting time to get into cardiac surgery. Bypass techniques and valve reconstructions were becoming more refined. Heart-lung machines, first developed in the 1950s, had revolutionized heart surgery by keeping blood and oxygen circulating while surgeons operated on a still heart, an advancement that afforded surgeons more time and greater precision. Although they had evolved greatly, they weren't a perfect solution, and I wouldn't be able to save every patient. But I was quite sure that I could do some good as a cardiac surgeon.

I had reached another important decision by this point in my career, and that was to make yet another vow to myself—a commitment that I knew I must hold inviolable if I was to continue down this path. I would treat every patient in my care—young, old, black, white, rich, poor—as if that person were one of my own family, as if that life were as precious to me as Bhanu's had been. Over the coming years, it became a ritual of mine to remind myself of this promise every time I set foot in an operating room. Every life was dear, and I would give every patient my all. Anything less would not do.

twelve

CALIFORNIA BOUND

AMRIT, IN HIS TYPICALLY SKEPTICAL FASHION, urged me to reconsider my decision and content myself with being a general surgeon. By this time, Amrit had completed his own cardiothoracic training at Brown and had worked for a couple of years at Cape Cod Hospital in Massachusetts. Then he had moved to California to take over as head of thoracic surgery at the University of California, Davis Medical Center in Sacramento.

I didn't take offense at Amrit's attempts to dissuade me from pursuing cardiothoracic surgery, as I had with his comment years earlier about betting on a losing horse. I believed that by this point, he had seen that I was serious and dedicated to my career and that I could meet the intense demands of cardiothoracic surgery. Rather, I interpreted his cautiousness as big-brotherly concern. In his eyes, I was still the scrawny preemie, the fragile runt of the family who needed his protection and guidance. His own experiences, particularly the need to repeat so much of his training, were a constant source of irritation to him, and he had only wanted to spare me from similar hardship. His caution had no effect on me, however. I knew it would be hard to secure a spot in a cardiothoracic surgical residency program in the United States, but I was dead set on getting one.

I interviewed at many places, including Stanford, Tufts, Peter Bent Brigham Hospital, and the University of Utah. I nearly got into Yale. I was called back twice for interviews, where I met with Dr. Hillel Laks, an associate professor of cardiothoracic surgery who was one of the members of the selection panel. Dr. Laks was a fellow South African, born just five months after me in Pretoria. A Hasidic Jew, he had trained in Israel before coming to the United States to embark on what was shaping up to be an illustrious career. I was tremendously impressed during our interviews, and it seemed as if we were hitting it off. Ultimately I didn't get the position, because a resident who was already at Yale was given priority and he wanted the spot. But my encounter with Dr. Laks would later prove to have far-reaching consequences.

Case Western Reserve University in Cleveland, Ohio, offered me a position, and so did UC Davis, where Amrit was now working. This time around, I don't believe that his influence was the deciding factor in securing me an offer, as it may well have been back in Ireland. By this time, I had established a solid track record of accomplishments, and I felt certain that I was offered the position based strictly on my own merit.

I was once again at a crossroads, but this time I had two attractive options before me. Case Western was highly regarded, but I couldn't ignore the appeal of escaping a cold climate to live in sunny California. What settled it was the opportunity to work with Amrit. I had lost the brother who had been my closest friend, but now I had an opportunity to work alongside my brilliant eldest sibling, who had always been enigmatic to me. Amrit professed genuine excitement about the prospect of working together, and he urged me to choose UC Davis. It had long been his dream to reunite as much of our family as possible, and because he could no longer hope to make a triumphant return to South Africa, he appeared determined to make California our new home.

So in the end, it was an easy decision. I was bound for California.

I was sorry to leave Canada. I even wondered if I was betraying the country that had opened its arms to me and treated me with respect and dignity. The Canadian people I had encountered were as warm as the climate was cold, and the government had bestowed on me a security I had never before known by giving me refugee status and then landed immigrant status. I would always be beholden to this wonderful nation and filled with gratitude for everything it had given me.

But I had important reasons for wanting to pursue my medical career in the United States. For one thing, in the Canadian medical system, most cardiac surgeries were performed at university hospitals. It would have been difficult to establish a private surgical practice there, and I wanted to keep that option open. Also, my negative views of some aspects of the United States were softening. I had been angry about the Vietnam War, but by the time I left Canada, it was 1980, and America's involvement in Vietnam had ended several years earlier. Race relations remained problematic, and that, of course, concerned me. But I was gratified to see a growing protest movement in America against South Africa's apartheid policies, and I had spent enough time in the United States to appreciate that despite its flaws and messy politics, it was a nation that continued to evolve and strive to realize its ideals of liberty and equality, and that it was indeed a land of abundant opportunity for anyone willing to put in the hard work. I greatly admired the brash American can-do spirit and outspokenness. I knew that even a thin, dark-skinned, heavily accented son of a cobbler who had spent his first month in a shoe box and was raised in a society that deemed him unworthy of many essential human rights—even someone like that—could make it there.

In keeping with my philosophy of moving forward and always looking to the future, I indulged in no introspection—no what-ifs, no regrets, no looking back. At any rate, there was no time to ruminate. I completed my residency at Dalhousie on June 30, 1980, and in July, I moved to Sacramento and was off and running as a cardiothoracic surgical resident at the UC Davis Medical Center.

My days there were long and full. I would usually rise at 5:30 or 6:00 A.M. and start rounds with the senior or chief residents an hour later. My focus in the first year was on thoracic training, but we saw both cardiac and thoracic patients, including pediatric cases, sometimes babies just a few days old. One problem we'd see with newborns was patent ductus arteriosus: shortly after birth, an opening between two major blood vessels leading from the heart—the aortic and pulmonary arteries—usually closes off naturally, but occasionally, a large opening persists, which can lead to heart failure if it isn't treated. Sometimes that calls for surgery.

No matter how routine the procedure, operating on babies requires nerves of steel and impeccable skill. Pediatric hearts are the size of walnuts, so tiny that there's quite literally zero room for error, and cardiac functions can deteriorate so quickly that there's often next to no time to react if a patient suddenly goes downhill. Alertness, speed, and precision are essential. During my training, the residents and cardiology fellows would stay on hand in the hospital for a long while after pediatric surgeries to ensure that if complications arose, they were dealt with posthaste.

Much as I admired the pediatric cardiac surgeons, the more I was exposed to that specialty, the more I was convinced that although I had learned to remain acutely focused and unruffled during surgery, working on children's hearts would be too stressful and exacting for me.

As a cardiothoracic surgical resident, I was also required to teach both medical students and general surgical residents doing their cardio rotations. I, in turn, would be taught by surgeons who were more experienced than I. It was like a trickle-down theory of knowledge, and it worked quite well.

Our rounds always took us to the intensive care ward first, where the senior surgeons would pepper me with questions. Once again, I found myself relying heavily on the nurses, who were knowledgeable and well informed about the patients and were always there to provide crucial backup to the physicians working on a case. After intensive care, I would check on other patients who were recovering from surgery, quizzing them carefully about how they were feeling and monitoring everything from urine output and blood pressure to appetite.

My surgical duties typically involved removing veins in preparation for cardiac bypass procedures. I would also help close up chests after surgery—a meticulous two-man job that requires wiring the sternum back together, closing up the subcutaneous layer, and then suturing the outer layer of skin. Sometimes I'd be called upon to put in the Swan-Ganz catheter, a thin tube inserted into the right side of the heart and the arteries leading to the lungs, which we used to monitor the heart and blood flow.

I worked on many lung and esophageal cases as well, performing duties such as ligating lobes. This involved tying off the blood supply and stapling the airway passage to the segment of the lung where the tumor originated. Then the tumor and surrounding lymph nodes would be sent to a pathologist for confirmation of a diagnosis.

One day I got a call from the chairman of the Department of General Surgery, who had an unusual task for me. An inmate at Folsom State Prison, about twenty miles from Sacramento, had been stabbed in the neck and brought in to the UC Davis Medical Center. I quickly assessed the situation and saw that the blade had punctured his superior vena cava, a big vein that goes to the heart, and that he was bleeding internally. I opened his chest, partially clamped the vein, and sutured it closed. Another five minutes and he would almost certainly have bled to death, but by that night, he was sitting up and talking. After that, I helped out on a few other cases from Folsom. Once I said something to the effect that I didn't know why these guys were so busy trying to kill each other. The senior surgeon replied that I shouldn't judge and that, at any rate, these prisoners were giving me good experience working with trauma. Point taken.

UC Davis also gave me my first experience of working on a particular type of trauma case that jarred me like no other. A patient who'd been shot in the chest had been admitted to the hospital, and I was called in to help. I flashed back to Bhanu, giving me a moment's pause. But I couldn't falter. By the time I'd arrived, his chest had already been opened, and his heart was still beating. The damage had been too great, however, and he didn't make it. I knew it was different than it had been with

Bhanu; this patient had been taken down by a single bullet rather than a spray of buckshot. I didn't know who he was or why he'd been shot. Still, it cut me to the core knowing that somewhere, someone would be grieving because of a single act of violence.

One aspect of a surgeon's job that I was learning to manage with increasing authority was knowing when—and when not—to operate. This is in some respects the most important decision of all. It's a myth that surgeons jump too quickly to surgery because that's all they know how to do. Indeed, I have always believed that a surgeon must be scrupulously cautious and thorough before deciding surgery is warranted. And as I proceeded in my career, more diagnostic tools were becoming available to help us make that decision. While I was at UC Davis, for instance, the gallium scan was introduced, giving us a noninvasive method primarily used to determine the progression of lung cancer and other cancers, so that we could make more accurate prognoses. Today we have scopes with tiny cameras that do the job even better.

Even after all my schooling and training, I still had to attend many didactic lectures. A few hours every week were devoted to a particular subject, such as congenital heart disease, or lung cancer, or different kinds of infections. Some procedures were technically difficult, and it was crucial to know every detail of anatomy and pathology as well as how to react in a methodical and timely fashion if the unexpected should happen. There was no way to bluff my way through any of it. I still had much to learn, so much of which I had to be aware at all times if I was to give patients my best.

I bought my first house in Sacramento, a three-bedroom midcentury tract home on T Street, two blocks away from the hospital, covering the down payment with money I'd made on the stock market thanks to some tips from the senior surgeons back in Canada. I made an exciting discovery when I rolled up the wall-to-wall carpets to find beautiful hardwood floors underneath. Even so, in buying this house, I was once again putting expediency first by choosing to live as close to work as possible. Amrit and most of the other faculty members lived in Davis, about fifteen miles west, where the main part of the university was located and the surroundings were more bucolic and agreeable than hot, muggy, charmless urban Sacramento.

I also purchased a new car, a Datsun 200SX, which I liked because of its sporty styling and because it was priced within my limited budget. I usually walked to work, but I used my new wheels in my scarce free time to drive to Amrit's place or accompany him on short trips to the Wine Country or to Lake Tahoe, Reno, or San Francisco. My brother introduced me to his social circle, primarily other faculty members, and I found that everyone was friendly and happy to include me in their get-togethers. Lunch would often be served to the thoracic surgical staff at the hospital, and it was there that I learned about the marvels of Mexican cuisine and that sublime wonder of nature, the avocado.

I was pleased that my relationship with Amrit was now one of equals—or near-equals, because technically he was my boss—and that we were at last growing closer. It wasn't the same easy, natural affinity that I'd had with Bhanu. I still found Amrit too rigid and traditional at times—much like my father—and he still chafed at some of my decisions and my irreverence regarding our native culture. But now we were in the same profession, working together, speaking the language of our trade. That common ground became the foundation of our deepening bond. He was long past his earlier misgivings about my aptitude for medicine and surgery, and he tried to be supportive—in his own way—of my ambitions. And I quickly observed that he wasn't just one of those book-smart guys who didn't perform well in the real world. In fact, he was an outstanding surgeon, technically as precise and skilled as they came.

One case in particular in which I assisted him stands out. A young woman had benign tumors in the lungs, stomach, and chest outside the esophagus, and we had to open up her chest and remove the tumors. I had never seen anything like this case before, and I wondered how many similar ones there might be. I discovered that her symptoms resembled those of an extremely rare condition called Carney's syndrome, named after the pathologist at the Mayo Clinic who had identified and written a paper about it. So I sent specimens to Dr. Carney, and he confirmed that our patient had indeed suffered from the same syndrome. Amrit and I wrote another paper to add to the body of knowledge, to tell other surgeons how to identify the tumors and to let them know that additional screening over a long period of time is needed to check for a recurrence of the tumors.

My new situation had other advantages. That year, I accompanied Amrit and other senior faculty members to a conference on thoracic surgery on Maui. It was my first trip to Hawai'i, and I was astonished by the lush beauty of the island. Amrit and I rented a car and toured around after our morning meetings, mesmerized by the kaleidoscope of tropical flowers and colorful birds and the blissfully warm trade winds. We visited a sugarcane plantation and went to a luau where a whole pig was roasted. I had my photo taken standing beside a young woman in traditional dress who had greeted me in the customary way by placing an orchid lei around my neck. I sent the picture to my sisters with the caption "This is the girl I'm going to marry."

I wasn't rich. Residents don't earn big money—at the time, I was pulling in an annual salary of $26,000. But that was more than enough back in the early 1980s, and I wanted for nothing. I also knew that my prospects were good and that I would be earning a lot more as my career progressed. Sometimes Amrit and I would tell each other how crazy it was to find ourselves living such a life, given where we'd started.

thirteen

COMPLICATIONS

I SHOULD HAVE KNOWN FROM PAST EXPERIENCE that smooth water never stays still for long. Inevitably complications arise, sometimes out of nowhere.

This time the facade of stability lasted only a few months. As a department head, Amrit had been privy to some troubling news: there were rumblings among the faculty that the cardiac part of the cardiothoracic surgical program was under sharp scrutiny because of high mortality rates, particularly with the coronary bypass cases that we were seeing more and more of at the time. I believed that the program was solid, but I suspected that we were seeing so many deaths at least partly because the senior surgeons were selecting so many high-risk cases.

About midway through my first year, the word came down. The American Council for Graduate Medical Education, an accrediting body for cardiothoracic programs, did not renew the accreditation for the UC Davis cardiac surgery department. And so the program was suspended from doing cardiac surgery until the problems could be fixed, a process that could take years.

It was a blow to many careers, mine included. I was to be left adrift halfway through my cardiothoracic surgical residency. Getting into another program for my final year was going to be extremely difficult. Even if I received permission to complete my training at another institution—something that the American Board of Thoracic Surgery frowned upon—openings would be even more scarce than they had been when I applied the first time around. Amrit urged me to apply everywhere I could think of, and I began contacting former colleagues and professors to see if they could help. I admit that I asked myself, more than once, *Should I have chosen Case Western Reserve?*

Strangely, though, I didn't panic. By that point in my career, I had encountered numerous obstacles and delays, yet I had always managed to jump through the hoops and find a way forward. I had cultivated relationships along the way, taken every available opportunity to do favors for colleagues, and demonstrated initiative by participating in research and getting papers published. All those factors would count in my favor. So I held fast to the conviction that it would all work out somehow. This was just a blip, and I would soon land on my feet.

My old professor Dave Murphy, who ran the dog lab back in Halifax, came up with an idea. H. Donald Hill, a former member of the Dalhousie faculty, was by then a celebrated heart surgeon at an institution in San Francisco that was then called Presbyterian Hospital, part of Pacific Medical Center. It had formerly been a part of Stanford University, but at that point in time, it was an independent and well-regarded hospital. Dr. Hill was accepting applications for a one-year cardiovascular surgical fellowship.

The program wasn't board certified, meaning that if I did the fellowship, I'd still have to complete the second year of my cardiothoracic surgical residency somewhere else. But it still had much to recommend it. In a profession filled with brilliant minds, Dr. Hill was one of the stars. He had been a protégé of Frank Gerbode, an internationally renowned surgeon and a pioneer in heart surgery. Dr. Gerbode had assembled a team that included Dr. Hill, and the group had developed innovative devices that significantly improved survival rates of cardiac and thoracic patients. After Dr. Hill took over the program, he continued the tradition of pushing the envelope in the adoption of new devices and techniques—in particular left-heart-assist devices and artificial hearts. I had no doubt that the fellowship would give me a highly valuable, and in many ways unique, experience, one that would make me more marketable to other cardiothoracic surgical programs. Furthermore, it would buy me time to land another spot where I could complete my residency. So I applied and got in. I breathed a sigh of relief.

During my last month at UC Davis, the faculty took the residents on a cruise up the Sacramento River to San Francisco Bay, where we crossed under the Golden Gate Bridge. The view was breathtaking, but I remember the outing mostly because a perfusionist, the guy who ran the heart-lung machine during surgery, sat on the edge of the boat and accidentally dropped his wallet in the water. He was ticked off, and although the rest of us were sympathetic, we couldn't help laughing at his misfortune. The cardiac program was suspended, but we still knew how to have a good time.

In July 1981, after just one year in Sacramento, I was on the move again. I sold my little house on T Street, loaded my belongings into my Datsun, and headed west.

San Francisco is only about a two-hour drive from Sacramento, so I knew there would be plenty of opportunities for Amrit and me to get together. Even so, I think he was sad to see me go.

My fellowship provided me with priceless training in cutting-edge surgical techniques with which I never would have had such broad experience if I had gone straight into the second year of a cardiac surgical residency program.

I learned every part of the heart-lung machine. Although these devices saved a great many lives, they carried their own set of risks and potential complications, particularly if patients stayed on them too long. Using the machines was like putting blood through a vigorous cycle on a washing machine; over time, platelets could become traumatized and coagulation factors damaged by all that whooshing around. Furthermore, it could produce bubbles that might migrate into the circulatory system and end up in the brain, triggering a stroke. So we learned to employ techniques to wean patients off these machines as quickly as possible.

I also gained much more experience working with intra-aortic balloon pumps, which improved the left-heart function of failing hearts. The balloon pumps were used in combination with drugs, but it was a constant juggling act to maintain that delicate balance so as to do more good than harm. Drugs like inotropes, for instance, were amazing in their ability to stimulate heart contractions, but they had to be administered with great care. Too much of these drugs could make the whole situation worse by overstressing the heart.

Dr. Hill provided me with my first exposure to what was then a relatively new technique for keeping the blood pumping in a failing heart. It was called the left-heart-assist device, a forerunner of the artificial heart, and Dr. Hill was an early adopter. Back in the 1980s, these devices were as big as grapefruits, and they had to be surgically implanted and connected to an external control unit the size of a small refrigerator. In some cases, they were used until the patient's heart recovered; in other cases, they provided temporary support while the patient awaited a transplant. They could be left in place for up to two years. This was especially helpful in the case of transplant patients, because donor hearts were so scarce.

I had been working with Swan-Ganz catheters since my residency in Canada, but I gained much more experience working with them in San Francisco. Invented in 1970 by two cardiologists at Cedars-Sinai Medical Center in Los Angeles, Swan-Ganz catheters greatly advanced the treatment of heart patients. This catheterization process involves inserting a thin tube into the pulmonary artery through the right side of the heart. A balloon on the tip of the catheter is inflated so that it will float into the artery, where it monitors heart function and blood flow.

Perhaps most critically, I was taught to read and interpret echocardiograms, which show the real-time function of all the chambers and valves of the heart. This gave me a crucial advantage in my later career, as I was able to stand my ground in discussions with cardiologists, who were responsible for analyzing test results and making diagnoses.

A certain amount of tension sometimes surfaces between cardiologists, who consider themselves the thinkers, and cardiac surgeons, who are sometimes viewed as little more than mechanics. But in my view, surgeons must know everything that cardiologists know and more. We are cutting cardiologists. And my expertise with echocardiograms has often helped me to make that case.

I was so thrilled to be a part of Dr. Hill's program that it never occurred to me to be bitter about my interrupted residency. His secretary arranged for me to stay in a hotel while I looked for an apartment, and I soon found the perfect place in a small building on Laguna Street, not far from the hospital, in the heart of the city. A one-bedroom unit with gorgeous wood floors and a large living room, it was the ideal spot for a single guy with a hectic schedule.

I adored San Francisco and its spectacular views of the bay and the Golden Gate Bridge. I visited art museums, took in concerts at Davies Symphony Hall, and enjoyed strolling through the diverse neighborhoods: Union Square, with its shops and restaurants; Haight-Ashbury, famous for its hippie free-love vibe; and the gay village known as the Castro. The annual Gay Pride Parade reminded me of a Cape Town event known as the Coon Carnival, in which minstrel troops wearing brightly colored clothing and lavishly decorated floats would pass by our shop on Sir Lowry Road. On weekends, when I wasn't working, I might visit beautiful Marin County, just north of the city. Sometimes in these tranquil moments, I allowed my mind to wander to thoughts of Bhanu, who would have loved this free and easy lifestyle, and I'd imagine conversations we might have had about our new lives in America. Then I'd shut down the impulse to dwell on what could never be. *Just get on with it,* I would tell myself.

For the most part, I was coming to appreciate the American society, culture, and political system more and more—in particular the principle of free speech, which is enshrined in the Constitution. In South Africa, everything had been suppressed and censored, and speaking out against the authorities was extremely dangerous. What a sharp contrast with the United States, where the free exchange of information and ideas is held sacred. To me, it was like a banquet to rival the copious portions of food Americans were wont to consume—a banquet that overflowed with open discussion on politics, culture, and controversial topics and in which daring to question the status quo was considered an inalienable right. I consumed it all with great gusto, filling up on newspapers and magazines, American television and films. By that time, impressive documentaries exposing the injustice of the South African political system were being widely distributed. It gave me some measure of satisfaction that at least the rest of the world was growing more aware of, and appalled by, the evils of apartheid.

Even so, I still believed that South Africa was beyond redemption. My bitterness hadn't dissipated, but I was determined to keep it locked away. I refused to live in the past or to open myself to disappointment over misguided hope that my native county would change for the better.

In those days, I rarely telephoned or even wrote letters to my father. I knew that any conversation with him would turn to admonishments about my failure to settle down and marry a tradition-minded Indian girl. And I was still nursing my anger at his coldness after his remarriage and his refusal to help me through medical school. Mostly, though, I still seethed over his comments after Bhanu's death. My brother had been shot in cold blood, and all my father could do was question why Bhanu had a store in that area, why he went down to the street during the rioting. I had managed so far to keep my wounds covered. I didn't need my father to pick at the scabs.

I did write frequently to Dhiraj and to Padma and Hansa, who were all still in South Africa. My younger half siblings were still there too, but we weren't much in contact back then. In 1979, Padma, who had also resisted the pressure to enter an arranged marriage, had wed a man of her own choosing. Still holding fast to my vow never to return to South Africa, I didn't bend even to attend the wedding, nor did I go back in 1981, when the first of

Padma's two children was born. Amrit, meanwhile, continued to beseech all our siblings to move to the United States and to research legal means of enabling them to do so.

He had good reason to worry. The brutality in South Africa was as bad as ever, and we continued to fear that a huge race war was coming. In September 1977, one year after Bhanu's death, the activist and student leader Steve Biko, founder of the Black Consciousness Movement and an anti-apartheid icon, died from injuries he had suffered while being held by the police. After he was killed, the violence and tension ratcheted even higher; in some parts of the country, tanks rolled down the streets on a daily basis. People in our community were frightened, my sisters included. Bhanu's death had proven to them that no one was safe, that the killing of innocents was just business as usual under apartheid. Yet for reasons I couldn't quite fathom, they were still reluctant to leave.

fourteen

CITY OF ANGELS

AS SOON AS I LANDED IN SAN FRANCISCO, I hit the ground running to secure my next position.

It wasn't a given that I'd get in anywhere. First I had to contact the American Board of Thoracic Surgeons to ask if they would acknowledge my second year of cardiothoracic surgical training at a different institution from the one where I had started. The board normally would have frowned upon splitting up the two years, but because the collapse of UC Davis's cardiac program had left me no choice, they made an exception in my case.

Next I had to find that rare opening for the single year's worth of training that I needed. Once again, I put out feelers to friends and former colleagues and sent out at least twenty applications. I received expressions of interest from the Albert Einstein College of Medicine in New York and from the University of British Columbia. But before I could pursue those possibilities, I received a phone call that would change my life.

Back when I had first applied for a cardiothoracic surgical residency, I had nearly landed a spot at Yale, but I was understandably passed over for an applicant who was already a resident there. I was disappointed at the time, but I felt I had established a certain rapport with one of the surgeons who had interviewed me, Dr. Hillel Laks.

125

Not long after that, Dr. Laks had been lured away to head up the cardiothoracic surgery program at the University of California, Los Angeles. It was a real coup for UCLA to land someone of his stature and a sign that the university, already one of the top institutions of higher learning in the world, was putting a priority on building up its cardiothoracic department.

I hadn't been mistaken about my feeling that Dr. Laks had seen some potential in me. Before he arrived at UCLA, only one cardiothoracic surgical resident was hired each year, but Dr. Laks wanted to expand the program and insisted that another resident position be added. And he wanted me for that spot.

Even with Dr. Laks pulling for me, it wasn't a slam dunk. I had to fly down from San Francisco and go through a series of interviews with other top staff members, during which I had to keep my nerves under control and hope I didn't blow it. Afterward, I drove in my rented car to Malibu and had lunch at a restaurant by the beach, where I saw so many pretty women that I hoped even more that I hadn't screwed up. Later I drove through the wealthy enclave of Bel Air and down the famous Rodeo Drive in Beverly Hills. I laughed and pinched myself, thinking, *What am I doing here?*

A few weeks later, I got the call. The position was mine.

I was overjoyed. I would be living in Southern California, where the weather and lifestyle were as agreeable as anywhere in the world. I would be training under a brilliant surgeon with a sterling reputation. And what could be better than UCLA? As a resident, I still wouldn't be making big money; my salary was a little more than $30,000 a year, and once again, I had no commitments beyond the one year. But by the end of that year, I would be among the surgical elite with some of the finest training available under my belt, so I had no worries about what I might do after UCLA. *At last,* I thought. *All my hard work and perseverance have paid off. I'm forty years old, and I'm finally at the top of my game.*

When I told Amrit, his response was "wow."

I couldn't wait to get started.

In June 1982, I loaded my possessions into a rented U-Haul truck and headed south.

It was a foggy day in Los Angeles. As I crossed over the Sepulveda Pass on the 405 Freeway, with Bel Air and Westwood on the left and Brentwood on the right, I saw through the mist the tall cypress trees lining the hillsides and was struck again by the abundant natural beauty of the Southern California landscape. I felt like a character in a movie about an unsophisticated bumpkin moving to this glamorous city of dreams. I could hardly believe that this would now be my home.

But I was well prepared to buckle down and focus on my work. I knew that my hours would be long and that I could be called into the hospital on a moment's notice, so as was my custom when choosing my lodgings, I decided to live as close to the UCLA Medical Center as possible. I settled on a one-bedroom apartment at the intersection of Sunset Boulevard and Barrington Avenue, just a stone's throw from the UCLA campus.

Just as before, my days began early with rounds at the hospital, starting in the intensive care ward then on to the telemetry unit, where patients who were stable enough were moved after the ICU. After that, I'd be in the operating room, usually assisting on two or three surgeries a day. Demanding as the surgical work could be, it had been impressed upon me throughout my training that post-operative care was equally critical. Here, again, the nurses were invaluable assets, and I made it a point to cultivate good relations with them and make certain that they understood what to do and what problems to watch for, whether it was blood pressure that was too high or too low; signs of internal bleeding, stroke, or infection; or a thousand other possible complications. I was scrupulous about monitoring post-op patients, because ultimately, the responsibility for what happens after an operation lies with the surgeon, who is like an orchestra conductor, coordinating every instrument.

The stakes were high. If a patient went sour after surgery, back to the operating room we might go to fix the problem, which often meant the difference between life and death. On rare occasions, there wasn't time even to make it back to the OR, and we would open up a patient's chest and go back in right there in the ICU. There was never the luxury of time; decisions had to be made in an instant, and they had better be right. It might seem obvious, but it's worth stating: for a surgeon, there's absolutely nothing worse than having a patient die on your watch.

I well remember one of my first cases. I was assisting on an operation to remove a lung from a cancer patient. He had presented as an acute asthmatic attack, but the lead surgeon said there had to be something more to it, and sure enough, we found a tumor. The surgery went well, but in the middle of the night, the patient's blood pressure dropped precipitously, he went into respiratory distress, and I was called back in. I inserted a Swan-Ganz catheter into the pulmonary artery, and the patient stabilized. When he was ready to be discharged from the hospital, he was so grateful that he handed me and everyone else who had worked on his case a hundred dollar tip.

I had other responsibilities as well. Because I was a senior resident, I taught a lot, bringing junior residents, interns, and medical students along on rounds to discuss cases. I also spent one day a week in the clinic examining patients who had been released and were back for postoperative checkups. One evening each week we'd devote to faculty members' case presentations, including presentations by clinical faculty members from the community who were employed elsewhere but remained affiliated with the university.

No matter how late it got, I could never leave the hospital without checking on patients during evening rounds and preparing for the next day's cases. Some nights I'd return home late, sleep four or five hours, and then be back to work again, knowing that I had to be sharp and in control at all times, because so many things could, and sometimes did, go wrong—and when complications arose, I needed to act quickly and decisively. The stress was brutal, the hours insane, and the mental demands extraordinary. I was working like hell, and I loved every bit of it.

It didn't take me long to realize that my mentor, Dr. Laks, was an honest-to-God genius, undeniably the greatest surgeon with whom I have ever worked. Observing him in action, I was astonished at the way he took on the most complex cases and turned them around. He saved children on their death beds.

He was always pushing the envelope with more advanced and refined surgical techniques and was flat-out brilliant at congenital heart cases—those in which defects are present at birth. In one case involving a baby with congenital heart disease, he developed a technique to improve upon the use of pulmonary artery banding, a method to reduce excessive blood flow to the lungs.

Imagine a pair of pajama bottoms with a string to tighten or loosen the fit around the waist. That same principle was applied to an adjustable snare, or band, that could be installed around a shunt and used to control the amount of blood flowing to the lungs. It was a terrific idea that worked beautifully, and Dr. Laks, another colleague, and I ended up cowriting a paper on the technique. Dr. Laks was renowned for his work with such congenital defects as cyanotic heart, in which the blood oxygen is low. This requires an intricate restructuring of the architecture of the heart to redirect blood flow. I would see him operate on these so-called blue babies, and by the time they were taken off the heart-lung machines, they would be pink. Pink! Or he would correct the hearts of babies born with one ventricle instead of two, a condition that would otherwise be a death sentence. His technical skills were phenomenal, his knowledge of anatomy and pathology impeccable, and his insight into the human body almost uncanny.

Dr. Laks was a terrific teacher too, which I found rather amusing given that he was actually a few months younger than I. He was mild mannered and meticulous—I never once heard him shout or lose his cool—but during surgery he'd sometimes scowl, which was the signal that I wasn't doing something to his exacting standards. I found this quirk endearing and an effective means of getting me to hone my skills further. Above all, I wanted to avoid making Dr. Laks frown.

Yet he would never boast, even after performing yet another miraculous surgery. "Don't worry, Himmet," he'd say. "You'll be able to do it too. It's just experience."

Needless to say, I liked him a lot, but my respect for him was beyond measure.

UCLA was an unbelievable institution, and I was amazed by the resources at our disposal and the amount of cutting-edge research being conducted by some of the top minds in our field. I was fortunate to work with many other brilliant surgeons while I was there, including Gerald Buckberg, a renowned researcher whose pioneering work on techniques for protecting the heart during surgery are used by surgeons all over the world, and James V. Maloney Jr., who had performed the first open-heart surgery west of the Mississippi at UCLA in 1956 and was the chair of the Department of Surgery—Dr. Laks's boss—by the time I came onboard.

At first I would only assist the more senior surgeons, but as Dr. Laks grew more confident in my skills, he allowed me to take the lead on cases, gently instructing and testing me along the way. His ability to handle the most complex cases was astounding, but he also impressed upon me the importance of something as seemingly routine as suturing. Stitches must be perfect, he insisted—not too deep, nor too shallow, and spaced as correctly as if a machine had put them in. It was the Goldilocks principle in action: Only stitches that were just right would do.

As time went on and Dr. Laks's trust in me grew, he even paid me the compliment of asking if I'd be willing to go to Australia for another year of training on pediatric hearts. I was grateful for the vote of confidence, but I turned him down. Not only was I dead certain that operating on kids would be too nerve-wracking even for a steady-handed fellow like me but I was starting to long for an end to my wandering ways. I had spent two decades on my education and training, and I was no longer a young man. I wanted to put down roots and, if I should be so lucky, find a woman to settle down with and finally have a family of my own.

During my residency at UCLA, I once again had to figure out what would come next. I didn't expect that I'd be hired on permanently; it was the common fate of residents to hear "good-bye and good luck" once their training was completed. That was a fact of life that I took in stride, and so I began applying for positions at other institutions.

Then an amazing thing happened: Dr. Laks asked me to stay on and join the faculty at UCLA. As an assistant professor, I would be on the lowest rung of academia, below the associate and full professorships that took years to achieve. But still, I was in, and I couldn't have been happier.

At the end of my residency, a ceremony was held for me and the other cardiothoracic surgical resident who was completing his term. It wasn't a formal graduation, more an unofficial acknowledgment of our achievements and a chance to poke fun at us. Indeed, the faculty put on a skit in which they mercilessly lampooned the two of us. I was skewered in particular for complaining about the faraway parking space I'd been allotted, and I nearly fell on the floor laughing when I saw the T-shirts they'd had made, which read, "My Parking Spot."

Now that I was a faculty member, I was all business. After my years of studying, training, and working diligently to get to this point, I understood perfectly what an enormous responsibility I had been given, and I couldn't afford to become puffed up with my own sense of self-importance. Lives would be entrusted to me, and if I screwed up, the consequences would be dire. I was more serious, more tightly controlled than ever, and I knew that doing my best would take more than just using what I had already learned. I had to keep educating myself and stay on top of every new discovery and technique so that I could give my patients the very best care.

Those were heady days of cardiothoracic surgery at UCLA. The field was evolving rapidly, and the university was striving to cement its reputation as one of the world's best. As an assistant professor, I took my orders directly from Dr. Laks, who organized the teaching roster and divvied up cases referred by cardiologists. Coronary bypasses, pacemaker installations, even some lung cases—they would all come my way. Even though I was receiving more of my own cases, I would still step in to assist as needed, opening up and closing chests for Dr. Laks and other more senior surgeons. I also assisted the research fellows at the university with their lab work, which was a good way of staying current with the latest research. Laks would assign me subjects to cover in lectures and send residents and students to me for instruction.

I impressed upon them, as had been impressed upon me in my own training, the importance of thoroughly examining both preoperative and postoperative patients. Some doctors become complacent and resort to cursory exams, but as a teacher, I wasn't about to let that happen under my watch. A complete exam takes time, but it's crucial to go through each step meticulously. Before surgery, tests and monitors must be checked for any red flags, and the surgical team must continually discuss how each patient should be treated given his or her particular needs and concerns. When following up on postoperative patients, I taught my students to ensure that they went through the entire checklist of measurable factors, monitoring blood pressure, heart rate, urine output, and so forth. I also instructed them to look patients directly in the eyes and to pay attention to such troubling signs as a weak handshake, clammy skin, or slurred speech.

Sometimes I was sent to work on cases at the Veterans Administration hospital near campus, which was under the care of UCLA staff. And I diligently attended the weekly case presentations by faculty members and clinical faculty from throughout the Greater Los Angeles area. I found this an excellent way to enhance my knowledge of specific techniques and treatments and to learn about interesting and unusual cases. There is never a point at which surgeons know everything they need to know; the more we learn, the more we realize that the profession is an endless balancing act requiring myriad calculations along with some highly educated guessing. After all, no heart is perfectly healthy, but not every problem requires intervention. The mark of a good surgeon is knowing when the threshold has been reached—the point where doing the surgery is worth risking the many possible complications that could result. And once the decision to operate is made, it becomes paramount to do everything possible to minimize those risks and to deal with complications when they do arise. In many ways, being a cardiac surgeon feels much like gingerly treading on a frozen lake and hoping with each step that the ice doesn't crack.

Perhaps it was my intense attention to detail and follow-through that prompted Dr. Laks to ask me to write a manual on postoperative care. After I wrote it, he told me to give a copy to his boss, Dr. Maloney, for a critique. Dr. Maloney was amazed at the amount of effort I had put into making the manual comprehensive, and he distributed it to all the residents and nurses.

I was always on call. I kissed holidays good-bye; indeed, holidays are notoriously busy times for heart surgeons, because there are more accidents and people often experience higher levels of stress, which can lead to heart attacks and strokes. I often received calls on weekends or in the middle of the night. In those days before cell phones, we carried our beepers everywhere. If I was driving on a freeway and my beeper went off, I'd pull over to the shoulder at the nearest call box to phone in. If I was on a surface street, I would stop at a gas station with a phone booth. This was hard on my social life. Sometimes I would have to abandon a dinner party or a date in the middle of the meal.

In return for all this, I was suddenly earning far more money than I had ever made before. My salary was $90,000 a year, which I thought more than enough for a single guy with few basic needs. I also received medical malpractice insurance coverage, a despised but necessary fact of life for physicians, as well as travel expenses for attending lectures; an office; and, of course, medical insurance.

I saw little of the inside of my tiny apartment on Sunset Boulevard, and my leisure time was nearly nonexistent. I'd had a few short-term relationships with women I'd met through work, but none that stuck. Much as I wanted to get married and have my own family, I still hadn't found the right person, and I couldn't see how I could make the commitment anyway, given my rigorous schedule. Many surgeons I had known had ended up divorced, and that was an outcome that I absolutely wanted to avoid.

Sometimes I'd roll in to my little apartment late at night. I would pick up pizza or pasta at the takeout place next door, and as I waited for my order, I'd watch with amusement as Rolls-Royces and other fancy cars pulled up out front. Then I'd go home, eat my meal in silence, and fall into bed. I was too busy and too exhausted to feel my loneliness.

fifteen
SUDDENLY SOUGHT

BY NOW, BYPASSES HAD BECOME THE BREAD AND BUTTER of cardiac surgeons, but heart transplants were still rare. The first human heart transplant had been performed by Christiaan Barnard in South Africa in 1967, an operation that turned him into an international superstar.

But what most people outside of medicine didn't know at the time was that Barnard's success was built on the work of many others, most notably a group of American researchers. Chief among them was Norman Shumway, who had achieved the first successful heart transplant, in a dog, at Stanford University in 1958. After Barnard's human heart transplant, the challenge became to find effective ways to keep the body from rejecting the donor heart. By the time I arrived at UCLA, immunosuppressant drugs, such as cyclosporine, had been developed and found effective at tamping down rejection and keeping transplant patients alive.

In 1983, Dr. Laks decided it was time for UCLA to venture into heart transplants. At the time, Stanford was the only institution in the state that had performed one, and so ours was to be the first in Southern California. In preparation for the procedure, I traveled with Dr. Laks to Stanford to learn the surgical techniques from Dr. Shumway and his colleagues.

Here's the second thing about heart transplants that most laypeople probably don't know: it's a relatively simple procedure, technically speaking. Bypass operations, by contrast, are far more difficult and complex and require working within the tiniest of margins. Transplants essentially involve suturing in a whole, intact heart—a far less intricate surgery than a bypass.

The tricky aspects of heart transplants involve the process of selecting both donor and recipient, the narrow window of time in which action must be taken, and the acute need for the highest level of postoperative care. That's why surgeons are just cogs in a very big wheel that also comprises an array of specialists, including a pulmonologist to work up the lungs, a nephrologist to check kidney function, a neurologist, a gastroenterologist, an immunologist, an infectious disease expert, and, of course, the cardiologist. Heart recipients must also undergo psychological and social screenings to ensure that they will take proper care of themselves after the surgery. All this requires careful planning and follow-through and some very critical decision-making.

In 1984, after we had undergone the training and received approval to proceed, a hospital patient was identified as a viable transplant candidate. Then it became a question of finding a donor heart, and when one became available, I flew with other members of the transplant team on a helicopter to McClellan-Palomar Airport in northern San Diego County to pick up the donor body and transport it back to UCLA. In those days, we took the entire body with the heart kept functioning through the use of a ventilator and medications. Back at the hospital, I helped Dr. Laks remove the heart and transplant it into our patient. I don't think it took more than two hours to perform the entire operation, and at first everything appeared fine: the patient came off the heart-lung machine without incident. But then she developed pancreatitis, and she died several days later.

Disappointed as we were, we tried to learn from the experience, and as time went by, Dr. Laks became one of the most prolific and successful transplant surgeons in the world. He also developed a significant advancement that saved many lives. In the early days, donor hearts were summarily rejected if they

Himmet during his UCLA days.

showed any level of coronary artery disease, which severely limited the number of hearts deemed suitable. But in a breathtaking display of his trademark genius, Dr. Laks decided that he could get around that limitation if he performed a bypass operation on the donor heart before transplanting it. His idea worked beautifully, particularly for older patients, and before long, it had become accepted practice.

As I continued my work at UCLA, I found myself suddenly quite in demand. After all my years of fighting for respect and working every angle imaginable to secure positions for myself, I was now fielding unsolicited job offers. I hadn't been actively looking for a new post, because I was very happy and considered myself incredibly fortunate to be working at UCLA. I was also reluctant to leave because of Dr. Laks, whose towering intellect and unequaled work ethic had influenced me so greatly. Nonetheless, I felt it was prudent at least to check out some of these offers and learn exactly what my options were.

One of the institutions that came knocking on my door was the big managed-care organization Kaiser Permanente, which was in need of a cardiac surgeon for its hospital on Sunset Boulevard in Hollywood. Kaiser was a determined suitor. I was offered a generous array of perks and a salary nearly three times what I was earning at UCLA.

Yet it wasn't the money that prompted me to give the offer serious consideration—not entirely anyway. I found the job attractive in part because of the way it was structured. I would be one of three cardiac surgeons on a rotating schedule, and all the Kaiser patients from throughout Southern California who were in need of heart surgery would be sent to us. The sheer volume of work would ensure that my caseload was always full. It was akin to a built-in practice. It would also guarantee that I'd be putting all my skills to use on every conceivable kind of heart problem, and after all my training, that was an appealing next step. If I were to set up my own practice one day—and given that I was already in my forties, that day would have to come soon—the experience juggling that kind of caseload would be invaluable.

One other consideration factored into my decision, and it was perhaps the most important one of all. There was no guarantee that if I stayed on at UCLA, I would earn tenure and be given a full professorship. This was no idle concern. Many people I had known had put in the required amount of time—typically seven years—before learning whether they had received tenure, and often the news wasn't good. Amrit was increasingly worried that he wouldn't be granted tenure at UC Davis, a prospect that added to his growing discontent over the direction of his career. Not for the first time, my brother's experience influenced my own career decisions, in this case, enough to tip the scale in favor of the Kaiser job offer.

The hardest part was telling Dr. Laks of my decision. He had taken a chance on me, and I was profoundly grateful for all the many ways he had helped me become a better surgeon. A gentleman to the core, he told me that I must do what I thought was right. He offered to provide me with a letter of reference should I ever need it, and he showed me great respect by asking me to continue on as a member of the clinical faculty. Although I have never regretted my decision, I do wonder sometimes what would have happened if I had stayed on at UCLA. Would I have received tenure? How much more could I have learned? Did I blow my chance to become a giant in my field, like Dr. Laks?

But I was never one to dwell on what-ifs. I had lived my life so far adhering to my philosophy of always moving ahead, never looking back, and I wasn't about to change. Besides, my ties to UCLA were not going to be entirely severed; as part of the clinical faculty, I would use every opportunity to give talks and present findings at the weekly meetings. I would be getting the best of both worlds.

At Kaiser, I became even more of a workaholic than ever. The three surgeons in our unit divvied up about one thousand hearts a year, allowing me to work on every kind of cardiac case imaginable.

Right from the start, I did whatever I could to set myself apart. I was as exacting as I could possibly be, even handing out the surgical manual I had written at UCLA to all the nurses.

One way in which I distinguished myself was by becoming the go-to surgeon for aortic aneurysms. An aortic aneurysm is an intricate, high-stakes operation that becomes necessary when the inner layer of the aorta tears or widens due to trauma, high blood pressure, or some other cause, leading to stroke, heart attack, heart failure, kidney failure, gangrene, or bowel ischemia. Scary stuff.

To perform the surgery, I would put patients on the heart-lung machine, stop the heart, drop the body temperature down to about twenty degrees Fahrenheit to protect the organs, drain out most of the blood from the body, cut the aorta, insert a Teflon graft, and suture it back together. Then the blood would slowly be returned. The whole procedure had to be done quickly but deliberately, and I had to work in perfect concert with the anesthesiologist and the perfusionist. Sutures had to be flawless, for if one were to give way, the aorta would bleed profusely. The patient could bleed to death or develop a postsurgical infection. Once the surgery was complete, the body had to be rewarmed very slowly to avoid releasing too much nitrogen into the blood and causing the bends. Many surgeons avoided these surgeries altogether because the risk of complications was so high. But I figured that if I could master aortic aneurysms, I could do pretty much any kind of cardiac surgery. The greater the challenge, the more alive I felt.

I was a man possessed, but in the best possible way. Working on tough cardiac cases was my drug. I was saving lives, and this gave me a feeling that was akin to ecstasy. Not that I gave any of this away to my patients or colleagues. I stayed just as buttoned up as ever. If the patient died, I would show no outward emotion, and if I saved a patient's life, I wouldn't strut about. I never panicked, not even in the most dire circumstances. Trauma or joy, either way I would downplay it and respond in the most composed manner possible—almost mechanical, really. But underneath all those protective layers I had so assiduously constructed, my own heart would rejoice in the intensity of the time I spent in surgery.

Consumed as I was with my job at Kaiser, I missed the academic environment and my former colleagues at UCLA, so I took every chance I could to present cases at the clinical faculty meetings. Two of these cases I remember vividly.

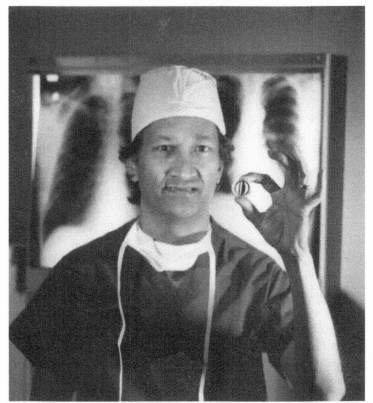

Himmet in surgical scrubs, standing in an operating room
holding a cardiac valve.

At that time, angioplasty—inserting a balloon into the
coronary artery to alleviate a blockage—was becoming more
commonplace. The first one had been performed in 1977 in
Switzerland, and use of the procedure proliferated. By the
mid-1980s, when I began working at Kaiser, many cardiologists
were learning the technique, with training typically facilitated
by the manufacturers. Often, complications ensued.

In those early years, the artery would sometimes shut down
again after angioplasty. This would happen because when the
procedure is performed, the plaque buildup that blocks the
artery is ruptured, and the trauma can cause the walls of the

artery to collapse. Or small cracks might open up in the artery, allowing plaque particles to enter the bloodstream and trigger a heart attack. As time went on, stents were developed to keep the arteries open following angioplasty. Later, drugs were injected into the stents to reduce clotting and scarring, leading to even better results.

But back in those days, we surgeons would sometimes find ourselves bailing out cardiologists when angioplasties went bad. Two cases that I recall in particular involved patients whose hearts had arrested, and the cardiologists were ready to throw in the towel. I quickly intervened. "No," I insisted, "take them to the operating room and let's give it a shot."

In both cases, there was not a moment to spare. Rushing through the corridors on the way to the operating room, my assistant and I took turns doing chest compressions to keep the heart beating until we could get the patient hooked up to a heart-lung machine. There, we quickly opened the patient's chest and performed bypass surgery, ever aware that we had to move as fast as possible, keep our wits about us, and not make any mistakes. When I think of these surgeries, an oxymoron comes to mind: controlled pandemonium.

Some surgeons might have been reluctant to operate in such circumstances, out of fear that even if the heart could be saved, the patient would end up brain-dead from lack of oxygen, and that would would look bad on the surgeon's record. There was also the fear that the patient would stay too long on the heart-lung machine, leading to other nasty complications. But I have always believed that a surgeon must do everything in his power to save a patient, reputation be damned. And I knew in these two cases that if I worked expeditiously, methodically, and decisively, I could do it.

Both patients woke up, recovered nicely, and went home.

I also handled some rare cases, such as tumors in the heart. Malignant cardiac tumors are typically metastatic, meaning that the cancer originated elsewhere in the body and migrated to the heart. These were generally untreatable. But in rare instances, we would see benign tumors that originated in the heart and blocked cardiac function. These were relatively easy cases, requiring us simply to cut out the mass. Even so, we had to be extremely careful and precise. If part of the tumor broke off and went to the brain, for instance, the patient could suffer a stroke. Even in the most straightforward cases, I took nothing for granted.

One day each week was devoted to post-op visits, and this was where many patients and their families would present me with gifts, such as bottles of wine, Scotch, or brandy. I was often asked if I was single, and the next thing I knew, my patients would be introducing me to their unmarried daughters. I never took any of them up on their thinly concealed attempts at matchmaking. Perhaps it was a reaction to my upbringing, but I was not at all interested in being set up. I would make my own choices when it came to female companionship.

One patient I'll never forget was a woman who was undergoing angioplasty when she started having chest pains. An electrocardiogram confirmed that she was experiencing ischemia, which is an inadequate blood supply to the heart, in this case caused by a tear in the left main artery. The situation required immediate surgery. The patient wanted to transfer to Cedars-Sinai Medical Center, which was world famous and was known as the hospital where Hollywood celebrities often went for treatment. I had to tell it to her straight: by the time she got to Cedars, she'd probably be dead—that's how urgent it was.

So she agreed to stay, and I performed a successful bypass surgery. She and her husband were so grateful that they invited me to their home for dinner after she recovered. When I arrived, my jaw nearly dropped. The house was like a palace, the food fit for a king, which was appropriate, because I discovered that my patient's husband was a highly successful jeweler with ties to royalty. They gave me a big brass clock and introduced me to their three daughters.

I never went out with any of the daughters, but I still have the clock.

When I took the job at Kaiser, I decided to buy a house. I chose a three-thousand-square-foot home with a pool, Jacuzzi, and two-car garage on Roscomere Road, just north of Sunset Boulevard, in the rarified enclave of Bel Air.

As Bel Air goes, the house was pretty modest. I knew that, except for sleeping, I wouldn't be spending much time there. I grew annoyed at the red needles from bottlebrush flowers that landed in the pool, but the fact was that I had little opportunity to go swimming anyway. One of the house's main attractions for me was the easy commute east on Sunset Boulevard to the hospital and its proximity to UCLA, where I still often visited. Buying it was just another one of the rather clinical, matter-of-fact decisions that I had become adept at making.

Even so, I couldn't quite believe my good fortune. I was living the dream. The dark-skinned kid from Cape Town who wasn't allowed to mingle with white people was now residing among the celebrity elite, driving each day down the Sunset Strip in my new Mercedes and stopping in for meals at the Beverly Hills Hotel's iconic Polo Lounge, the site of frequent star sightings. Sometimes I would chuckle to myself and wonder, *How the hell did this happen?*

One patient on whom I operated while I was still at UCLA was a wealthy Indian businessman who had ventured into the movie business. This man was so rich that when he traveled in India, he had an entire train car just for his clothes and servants. He'd had bypass surgery but then started to bleed internally. I fixed the bleed, and after he recovered, he befriended me, inviting me to his home in Santa Monica for dinner and to accompany him to lavish Hollywood parties where the drinks and drugs flowed freely. Through his circle of acquaintances, I was once invited to a film screening, followed by a private party at the famous male strip club Chippendales. I had been completely clueless about this kind of lifestyle, but it didn't take me long to realize that it wasn't for me. I've never seen so many beautiful women, but so many of them were high on drugs that it just made me sad. Besides, my work was my priority, and there was no way I was going to get distracted and jeopardize everything I had striven so hard to achieve. So after a few parties, whenever a similar invitation came my way, I politely declined.

Not that Los Angeles was all glamour and glitz. Early each morning, as I drove to work, I saw the prostitutes soliciting on the sidewalks. One night on my way home, I stopped at a gas station, and as I got out to work the fuel pump, two heavily made-up women in miniskirts hopped in the car and asked me if I wanted to "go out" with them. I managed to choke out a no, and they walked away leaving me dumbfounded, fuel pump in hand.

Mostly, though, I loved the LA lifestyle. I bought season tickets to the Hollywood Bowl, the famous outdoor amphitheater about which I had heard for years. The experience didn't disappoint. Picnics under the stars; cool, dry California nights; Beethoven and Tchaikovsky; even sometimes fireworks displays. I was mesmerized.

I also occasionally took in concerts at the magnificent Dorothy Chandler Pavilion in downtown Los Angeles. Sometimes I would visit Rodeo Drive in Beverly Hills, or I'd meet up with friends and head west on Sunset toward the ocean, stopping in at Will Rogers State Historic Park in Pacific Palisades for picnics while watching the polo matches played there. I loved walking along Ocean Avenue on the bluffs above the beach in Santa Monica.

But I was working like a dog, and such outings were rare. I soon realized that my purchase of season tickets for the Hollywood Bowl had been an exercise in wishful thinking. Parking was a nightmare; if I'd received an emergency call, it would have taken far too long to retrieve my car and get to the hospital. So I gave away most of my tickets. And when the Olympics came to Los Angeles in 1984, I longed to see some of the events, but I couldn't manage to get even to one.

I was so busy that I didn't dwell overmuch on a fact of my life in LA that, given my background, was a real sore spot. The areas where I lived, worked, shopped, and dined were mostly affluent, and predominantly white. In Bel Air, I rarely saw other people of color. I knew that other neighborhoods existed—the people I had known in Canada thought of Los Angeles as a city of gangs and violence—but I didn't even know where they were. I hadn't intended it, but I was living a privileged existence in a city where the economic, social, and racial divisions were stark. It wasn't apartheid, but most people stayed within the confines of their own isolated communities, and that bothered me.

At work I noticed that most of the other doctors didn't talk to other members of the staff, except on professional topics, and that troubled me too. I made a point of conversing with everyone, no matter who they were or what position they held. I once struck up a friendship with an X-ray technician who was African American, and he kindly invited me to his home in Watts to indulge in our shared interest in jazz. I didn't think twice about accepting, but I was surprised when I drove to his neighborhood in the south of the city to see that all the houses had iron bars on the windows. At my friend's home, I met his wife and family. We ate dinner, and they asked many questions about my life in South Africa. After our meal, as promised, we listened to jazz music. It was a perfectly delightful evening. Later when I told some other friends where I had been, they all told me I was crazy, that I could have been killed, and that I should never venture there again.

Their reaction was an eye-opener. It told me that racism is always there. Even if it's not written into law, it still lurks not far under the surface, rising up to show itself in everyday words and deeds. I had run away from South Africa because I couldn't stand to live off the crumbs of white privilege, but here I was in a different society where people often lived separately anyway and viewed each other with thinly veiled suspicion and contempt.

Perhaps Cape Town wasn't so far away after all.

sixteen

BREAKING A PROMISE

IN 1985, I BROKE MY PROMISE. I returned to South Africa.

My sister Hansa was getting married. I had missed Padma's wedding years earlier, and aside from seeing Amrit regularly and a short visit from Hansa when I was living in San Francisco, I hadn't spent any time with my family in nearly a decade—not since Bhanu's funeral. I thought long and hard about it but eventually relented, figuring I owed it to them to show my face. I decided I would make it a quick visit, in and out, and was determined not to let any of the toxicity of the country touch me. My world was different now, I was different, and I wasn't about to let myself slide back into that hole of insecurity and depression. Nor would I dwell on any of the cruel reminders of Bhanu's absence.

But my resolve was in danger of cracking on the day of the wedding, which was held at the house that Anjuli and Hansa still shared—Bhanu's former home. As is typical during any Hindu ceremony, incense was burning. At one point, a set of drapes near the incense urn caught fire, and I rushed to quell the flames. Then the flood of emotions came unbidden as I considered how close we had come to burning down the home of the brother who had sheltered and nurtured so many of us. He should have been there, on this day of all days, at the wedding of the little sister for whom he had cared so lovingly. But then, with my practiced stony discipline, I shut down the rush of grief as quickly as it had come upon me.

After being away so long, the racial tension felt even more pronounced. The wedding was in Cape Town, but afterward, Hansa and her new husband were to live in Uitenhage, a town near Port Elizabeth known for its big auto manufacturing plants, where conflict was rife and tanks rolled down the streets on a daily basis. The talk in my old community was about the coming revolution and what would happen to the Indians when the day finally came and the whole country went up in flames.

The sanctions imposed on South Africa, which by then had become an international pariah because of apartheid, were a frequent topic of discussion. Prices were skyrocketing, purchasing power was declining, whole industries were suffering, and the Indian merchants we knew were hurting right along with them. All my friends and relatives spoke of their fears, not just of a brutal uprising, but also of a complete economic collapse. Their anxiety was palpable.

But in other ways, nothing at all had changed, as if the old community were frozen in time, with the same parochial attitudes and disengagement from the rest of the world that had always disturbed me. Living in the United States, I had become accustomed to a vibrant, fast-paced lifestyle; a healthy, open exchange of viewpoints; and expectations of a better future. In South Africa, it was as if time just dragged on with nothing good to show for it.

People with whom I had grown up continued to treat me differently, as if I had some exalted status because I was a surgeon. I hated it. I wanted to shout at them, "I'm the same guy!" But I kept silent and tried not to cringe at their fawning. My father, predictably, started in on me the moment he saw me. "When are you getting married?" he demanded to know, to which I merely replied, "Someday."

And then my father did something completely surprising. At the wedding, he finally mended his relationship with Dhiraj. He accepted Belle, and astonishingly, the two of them later became good friends. Perhaps it was the sight of Dhiraj's three young children that melted my dad's resolve to shun his son. Maybe it was his reluctant realization that Dhiraj had turned out to be a good man, always gentle and soft-spoken, a devoted husband and father. Whatever it was, my father's sudden change of heart did nothing to soften my own disdain for his stubbornness. Years had been lost, and for what?

Before I'd left for South Africa, I'd contacted Dr. Bruno Reichart, who was at that time the head of cardiac surgery at UCT. I explained that I had acquired extensive experience with combined coronary bypass and valve surgery and offered to share my observations with members of his department, particularly my experience concerning the use of blood cardioplegia. This is a method of stopping the heart so that surgery can be performed while it is still and bloodless. The patient is given a cocktail of drugs that lowers the metabolic rate of the heart muscle, preventing cells from dying while there is no blood flowing through the coronary arteries. Dr. Reichart was welcoming, so during my visit, I gave my presentation at UCT, which I thought went very well.

Afterward, however, I was approached by an anesthesiologist who had been in the audience. He launched into a criticism of cardioplegia, saying that the technique was overrated and the results I had described were exaggerated. I kept my cool, but inside I was boiling. *Another South African jerk showing a total lack of respect to a nonwhite,* I thought. Perhaps I was too sensitive; perhaps my reaction was merely a reflexive response born of years of insults and degradation. But the episode confirmed what I already knew to be true. I was damned glad that this was no longer my country.

After my short visit, I returned to my real home, the one I had clawed and scraped to build for myself, where I could once again shut my mind and heart to the past.

Most surgeons at Kaiser considered the HMO a great stepping-stone. Many would stay for three to five years, bulk up on experience, and then leave to work in private practice. Almost from day one, I received offers, some attractive, others less so. The trouble was that most established practices wanted young physicians who would start at the bottom and serve as the workhorses of the business. At my age, I wasn't about to settle for grunt work. I wanted to call my own shots. So I talked to everyone who expressed an interest in me, considered each offer carefully, and did my due diligence.

In 1987, more than three years into my stint at Kaiser, the right opportunity came along. Fountain Valley Regional Hospital, a physician-owned community hospital in Orange County, just south of Los Angeles, was looking for a cardiac surgeon willing to be available twenty-four hours a day. I'd heard positive reports about the facility, and I was impressed with the doctors on the board who interviewed me for the position.

I also liked the deal they were offering. As an independent contractor, I would work in the hospital, but not strictly for it. It would be up to me to cultivate relationships with the cardiologists who were affiliated with the hospital, on whom I would depend for referrals. I liked the idea of being my own boss, and I felt confident that I'd have no problem proving myself with superior results. The hospital offered me a healthy stipend for the first two years just in case my initial income fell below a certain level. As it turned out, I didn't need it.

When I prepared for my move to Fountain Valley, I realized that this moment represented the culmination of everything I had worked toward my entire life. I was finally ready to settle down, in terms of both my career and my personal life. I had been dating a nurse anesthetist named Karen, whom I had met at Kaiser, and I began to imagine what life would be like with a family of my own. I was happy with my decision to establish my own practice as a community surgeon and grateful for the prospect of living out the rest of my life in beautiful Southern California.

But settling down didn't mean standing still.

I had no illusions about how difficult the path ahead would be. I was the new guy in town, and I would have to work tirelessly day and night to prove myself. For the first time, hearts wouldn't just come to me; I would have to solicit business. I needed to demonstrate that my surgical results were superior and that I could collaborate amicably with other professionals. In an industry as cutthroat as they come—one in which professional jealousies and petty disagreements could undermine a career—establishing good relationships and inspiring trust would be crucial.

Just to earn admitting privileges at the hospital, a proctoring surgeon was required to observe several of my surgeries and report on my competence. Finding another surgeon willing to do the proctoring was tough enough. Then, as fate would have it, my first proctored case turned out to be one of the most difficult surgeries to perform, a combined aortic valve triple coronary bypass operation. The surgery took five hours, and I had to work with an unfamiliar team. But fortunately, everything went smoothly; there were no complications, and afterward, the referring cardiologist sent all his cases to me.

Even so, I was taking a gamble that I could break into established circles and win the confidence of other physicians, particularly the cardiologists I needed to impress. Word got back to me that another cardiac surgeon had dismissed my prospects, saying, "Cardiac surgeons come and go. He'll only last six months."

As I had done my entire life, I set out to prove the naysayers wrong.

seventeen

MATTERS OF THE HEART

CURRICULUM VITAE IN HAND, I went door to door and introduced myself to as many doctors as possible, letting them know I was available should they need a cardiac surgeon. That first year, I shared an office and a secretary with a general surgeon, but it didn't take long for me to prove myself. I was known to be reliable; I got good results on even the most difficult surgeries; and I soon became well regarded for my postsurgical diligence. Before long, I was so busy that it made sense for me to set up my own office and staff in the building next to the hospital.

In fact, my workload increased so quickly that I soon realized I needed help.

Every cardiac operation is a team effort. In addition to the primary surgeon, there must always be another surgeon to assist and usually a general surgeon or physician's assistant to remove veins. There's the anesthesiologist, of course. A perfusionist operates the heart-lung machine and oversees an assisting technician who runs the cell-saver, which collects and filters the blood shed during surgery. Four nurses are typically required: the head nurse; another who helps with vein removal; a third to collect blood swabs and tissues for the cell-saver and to count instruments and swabs to ensure nothing goes missing; and a fourth nurse on hand to fetch extra needles, surgical patches, or blood products for transfusions.

It's a lot of people, but each person serves a vital purpose. In fact, it's important to have as few people working a surgical case as possible, for every additional body in an operating room raises the risk of infection. Also, it's critical that everyone remain as still as possible during surgery, for even though operating rooms are sterilized, it's impossible to remove every dust particle. Any movement could stir those stray particles, causing them to migrate unseen into the surgical field, raising the potential for problems down the road. As I operated, classical music played quietly in the background to keep me calm. Often the only other sounds were the clinks and clanks of our surgical tools and the beeping of monitors. I avoided idle talk, instead relying on intricate nonverbal communication facilitated by frequent eye contact with my colleagues. The tiniest change in expression could alert me to something that needed my attention.

So I was keenly aware that a surgeon like me could never be a lone wolf. My success would depend in no small measure upon the people who surrounded me. As my practice grew, I needed a partner I could trust, a surgeon with excellent skills and integrity who would back me up and who had my best interests at heart.

I knew just the person.

My big brother Amrit by this time had been working at UC Davis for about seven years. He was a top-notch surgeon, but he had endured a number of disappointments and setbacks in his career. He had always been the brilliant one in the family, the high achiever, but for reasons I couldn't explain, he had never become board certified in cardiothoracic surgery. Board certification, which involves a testing and peer review process, is intended to demonstrate a physician's level of expertise in a specialty. Although it is technically voluntary—many excellent doctors I've known never became board certified—not having this credential can limit a physician's career opportunities.

What's more, Amrit's fears about not making tenure had materialized. Already in his mid-fifties, he was ready to move on to a new position. For the first time in my life, rather than me needing my brothers' help, I was now in a position to help one of them. I saw it as a win-win, but I also understood that this new relationship might be difficult for Amrit to accept. Always a bit prickly, my brother might be irked if he felt that he'd only be playing second fiddle to his little brother. The last thing I wanted was to further damage his pride after he'd already suffered so many unlucky breaks in his career. I had to be diplomatic. We would be helping each other, I told him, and the fact was that this was absolutely true.

He accepted my offer and joined me in my practice in Orange County. The Dajee brothers were together again.

About two years after I started my practice, I at last completed my journey to becoming the person I had always wanted to be.

One day, I drove to downtown Los Angeles, parked my car, and strode into a section of the cavernous convention center where a few hundred immigrants like me were gathered. I had to take a test. The questions were simple, but I didn't want to leave anything to chance, so I had studied the preparatory pamphlet in anticipation of questions such as, Who was the first president? How many states are in the United States?

The people congregated there formed a great hodgepodge of ethnicities and backgrounds, yet we were all there for the same reason, and that bound us together. I submitted the required paperwork, answered more questions in a brief interview, and, when the time came, stood among the crowd and held my hand up, swearing allegiance to the United States of America and pledging to obey its laws and defend its Constitution.

It's hard to explain how momentous this oath felt to me. It's something that perhaps only another naturalized citizen could fully understand. Against some long odds, I had achieved much in my life so far. But nothing, not even my medical degrees, could compare with this accomplishment. It was the most singular achievement, the greatest moment of my life, the point at which I finally felt that I had well and truly made it. I was a citizen of the

United States of America, with all the rights that status accorded, and with the strength and dignity of the entire nation to support me. I was free, and I felt as if anything would be possible from that day forward.

If there had been a bonfire in front of me, I would have thrown my South African passport into it.

During my first year working in Fountain Valley, I had rented an apartment in Newport Beach, an affluent community popular with doctors that was only a fifteen-minute drive from the hospital where I worked.

Newport Beach, a beautiful coastal community with a blissful climate, is pretty close to paradise. The city is also one of the wealthiest in the country. It is home to many celebrities and the moneyed elite, who own luxurious waterfront houses situated alongside the bay or on one of the many small islands dotting the gorgeous harbor. I hadn't known a single soul when I moved there, but I found my neighbors to be friendly. I was pleased with my choice, even though I would have little time to enjoy my splendid new surroundings.

In fact, I was ready to settle in for the long haul, and I decided to buy a house. My practice was doing well, I had saved wisely, and I had learned early on from my father that buying property was a sound investment strategy. But not just any house would do. After years of living alone, I was feeling a hollowness in my life. I longed to get married and have children, so I wanted a place with room to grow. Living right by the water wasn't an option, because it would have added too much time to my commute, and as a surgeon on call, those extra few minutes could be crucial. I needed a home with easy access to the nearest freeway.

When the real estate agent showed me a house about a mile and a half inland—in the area known as Pill Hill because of its high population of physicians—with pillars and a winding staircase and an ocean view that evoked memories of Cape Town, I knew in an instant that this was the place for me. Amrit thought I was crazy for buying a roomy two-story house with four bedrooms and another swimming pool that I might never use. But I knew what I wanted, and I was certain it would prove to be a good decision.

I had my heart set on something else, as well. At this point, I had been dating Karen, the nurse anesthetist I had met at Kaiser, for about four years. It had been the longest relationship of my life so far. When I had first met her, I had been attracted by her compassionate way of interacting with patients and by how dedicated she was to her job. We would spend what little free time I could manage together, going to see movies or occasionally to the beach for barbecues, and we once took a two-week trip up the coast all the way to Vancouver. But my busy surgical schedule meant that our relationship always came in a distant second to my career, and for quite some time, I'd had a sense that something was off between us. She sometimes wouldn't answer her phone when I called, and she had started to give me evasive answers about what she had been doing.

Yet I so badly wanted to get married that I put aside my misgivings. I summoned up my courage, and one day, at my big new house, I asked Karen to marry me.

She said no.

It's strange to think that a no-nonsense cardiac surgeon could have his heart broken. It was as if I'd been bludgeoned in the chest, so deep was my hurt. I had become so entangled in the idea of being in a loving, committed relationship and so certain that the timing was finally right to get married that I had stumbled ahead blindly without really stopping to consider whether that was what Karen wanted, or if I had chosen the right person on whom to stake my dreams.

Looking back not long after the breakup, I was grateful that she turned me down. Once I got past the pain of rejection, I realized that she had done me a great favor. Our relationship hadn't been on solid ground for some time, and being honest with myself, I admitted that it never would have been, even if we had stayed together. I had always promised myself that if I married, it would be forever, and if I wasn't completely certain,

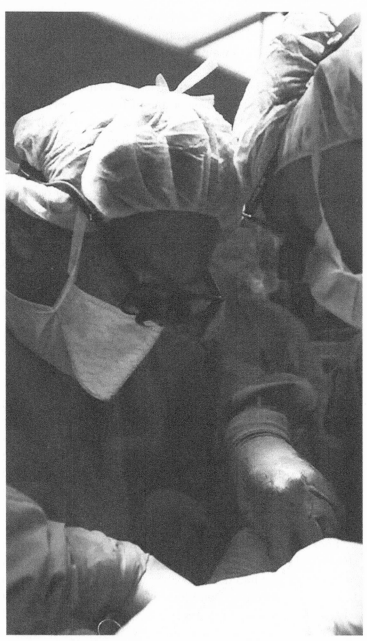

Himmet performing open-heart surgery.

then I would reconcile myself to a life alone. I would be married to my work, and that would be enough.

So that was how I dealt with it. I threw myself into my practice ferociously, taking on more, and more difficult, cases than ever. The operating room was my sanctuary, the place where I felt at once both exhilarated and calm. Other people turn to drugs and alcohol. But for me, the best diversion from my anguish was to cut deep into patients' chests and then see them come back to life. I never wavered from my philosophy of treating my patients as if they were family, often staying with them for hours to make sure nothing went wrong and then calling to check on them again after I arrived home, no matter how late.

I was at the pinnacle of my career, and I was in control of everything. I had a secretary to handle my packed schedule and a billing specialist to deal with my finances, and I had hired a consultant to help me learn how to build and manage my practice. I gave lectures to the staff at Fountain Valley; stayed current with new techniques and devices by attending seminars, workshops, and conferences; kept going to meetings at UCLA; continued to cultivate relationships with other doctors; and, after a time, won admitting privileges to other nearby hospitals. My focus was as sharp as ever.

No regrets. No looking back. I forged ahead as I always had, determined to live my life on my own terms.

I had kept my emotions in check for as long as I could remember, through disappointments, rejection, and tragedy. My hands had stayed steady and my mind alert every time I operated. I accepted patients whom other surgeons wouldn't touch, vowing to use everything I had learned to find a way to keep their hearts beating.

But all of this had taken a silent, unseen toll, until one day, I found that it was my own heart in need of healing.

It was July 1991, several months after my breakup from Karen, and I was forty-nine years old, still living alone, still working like a madman. One night at about one in the morning, I was suddenly awakened by chest pain. It wasn't crushing pain—about a three or four on a scale of one to ten—but it was steady and strong, and it ran up my shoulder to my jaw and all the way down my left arm. I checked my heart rate, and it was a little fast. I knew exactly what was happening. A heart attack would have been much more severe, but the signs of reduced blood supply were clear. Something was wrong with my heart.

By the time I would normally have awoken and readied myself for the day, the pain had subsided, but I knew better than to ignore the episode. That morning, I headed north to Los Angeles, Amrit accompanying me, to be seen by my former colleagues at UCLA. My lab work was normal, but my symptoms were classic angina, the kind of chest pain that signals coronary artery disease. A cardiac catheterization was ordered, a procedure that involved inserting a thin, hollow tube into my groin area and passing it through the aorta. Then an angiogram was performed, during which a dye was injected through the catheter so that any blockages would show up on images.

The culprit was revealed. There was an obstruction in my left anterior descending artery, or LAD—otherwise known as the widowmaker. If that artery is 100 percent blocked, the patient is likely to die suddenly from a heart attack, aneurysm, or ventricular arrhythmia. Mine was about 70 percent blocked, serious enough to require immediate intervention.

My team of doctors, including Dr. Laks, decided that I should undergo angioplasty, a common procedure involving a special catheter with a balloon on the end. The balloon is inflated at the site of the blockage, squashing the plaque into the artery wall to increase blood flow. During the procedure, I started bleeding into my groin and lost about a pint of blood. I was sedated but still awake at the time and was aware of what was happening. Yet I didn't panic. I discussed it with the physicians treating me, and we decided that the bleed could be managed through medication, but it left me with a distinctive limp for a few days.

The doctors at UCLA made another crucial discovery: I had diabetes and high cholesterol. I was still as skinny as I'd always been, but the diagnosis should have come as no surprise, because there is a high incidence of diabetes among Indians, and it often leads to coronary artery disease. My father was diabetic; so were many of my cousins. I was pretty much genetically programmed to get the disease, and my stressful lifestyle certainly hadn't helped matters.

At least in my case, the old adage about doctors being poor patients is true, because I certainly hadn't followed the advice I routinely dispensed to my own patients. I hadn't taken adequate care of myself and never went for checkups—that was why my diabetes had gone undiagnosed. I'd considered myself invincible, and now I'd had a big warning sign. I was damned lucky I hadn't dropped dead.

But I wasn't out of danger. I stayed at UCLA for three days, and just two days after my discharge, I was back again with more chest pain.

An angiogram showed a tear in the plaque that lines the artery, which meant there was a risk of a complete blockage. It was decided that I'd be treated with medications and would return in early August for a stress test. That test went fine, but not long afterward, the pain returned. This time I went to a hospital closer to home to find that the left anterior descending artery had narrowed by 50 percent. I called Dr. Laks, and he agreed that surgery was now warranted. He would perform the operation scheduled for a month later.

But my heart had other ideas. In late August, before my scheduled surgery, the pain came on again. Dr. Laks was out of town, but after talking it over with Amrit and my cardiologist, I knew I couldn't afford to wait. A couple of surgeons at a local hospital performed a total of five bypasses on my heart.

As I recovered, I knew I would have to make some lifestyle changes. Healthy eating, exercise, and regular medical checkups would have to be top priorities. Above all, I needed to reduce stress. But after a lifetime of pushing myself to the limit, that wasn't going to be easy.

A month after surgery, I was back at work.

eighteen

A DAY I NEVER FORESAW

AS I PUT DOWN ROOTS IN CALIFORNIA, I continued to keep a close watch on what was happening in my native country, and I was astounded at the course of events. The dominos had been falling for some time, but by the late 1980s, the pressure against the apartheid regime was insurmountable. International sanctions and internal unrest had taken a severe economic toll on South Africa, and the collapse of the Soviet Union meant that the United States and other Western governments no longer saw any reason to consider the Afrikaners a bulwark against communism. The threat of civil war was as acute as ever.

South African prime minister P. W. Botha had resigned in 1989, and his successor, F. W. de Klerk, made a surprising announcement in his opening address to Parliament in February 1990. He said that he would lift the ban on the ANC and other liberation organizations, ease restrictions on the press, and release political prisoners. Shocked as I was at these concessions, I still wasn't buying it. I knew that the Afrikaners must have something up their sleeves, that they would never willingly cede an iota of control or show an ounce of compassion or decency.

And then came the bombshell. On February 11, 1990, Nelson Mandela, who had been imprisoned for twenty-seven years, was freed. After his release, he began advocating for peaceful change and started working with the government to draw up a new constitution. Within a few years, the new constitution, the product of compromise, took effect, and in 1994, elections were held that led to a coalition government with a nonwhite majority. Mandela became the first black president of South Africa.

It was a day I thought I would never see. Even as the Afrikaner-led government was crumbling, even after Mandela was set free, and even when the system of apartheid was being dismantled, I remained skeptical. So deep was my mistrust of the whites in South Africa that I was certain they had some backdoor scheme to cling to power. And as apartheid was officially coming to an end, I still believed that the entire country would collapse into a fiery race war that would make all the previous violence look tame by comparison.

But I was wrong. Totally wrong. Never have I been so happy to be so. I could only marvel later at the behind-the-scenes negotiating that must have taken place, and the desperation of the whites who feared a bloody uprising, that must have impelled the government to accept such revolutionary change. I credited Mandela, my boyhood hero, for his ability to keep the public calm and negotiate a deal with the very people he'd had every reason to hate and mistrust, those who had unjustly persecuted him and imprisoned him for decades. He understood that bigger issues than retribution were at stake and that if he didn't quell the violence and work with the Afrikaners, institutions would crumble and the entire country would devolve into chaos.

As the situation was unfolding, I was relieved that Padma and Hansa would be safe. It had long been Amrit's dream to reunite our family, and at last he had partially succeeded by helping our sisters obtain green cards so they could join us in America. In late 1991, Padma and her husband and two children emigrated to the United States and moved into my big house in Newport Beach, where they stayed for about a year and a half before moving to a place of their own. A few months after Padma left South Africa, Hansa followed, along with her husband and daughter. She and her family moved in with Amrit—who by this time was also married with children—for a short time before they too settled into their own home nearby.

But I worried constantly that my remaining family and friends in South Africa, particularly my father and Dhiraj and his wife and kids, would be caught up in the violence that I was certain was inevitable. Miraculously, Mandela managed to hold the country together. Again, I was happy to be wrong.

In the middle of all this change, in October 1992, I decided to take another trip to South Africa. My brush with death had given me a sense of my own mortality. None of us was getting any younger, and I felt the need to see my father, Dhiraj, and other family and friends. I was well enough to make the trip; indeed, I reasoned that a break would do me good.

Upon my arrival in Cape Town, I was astounded by how much had changed in the seven years since my last visit, to see people of different races walking the streets side by side. Yet, despite the progress, violence remained an everyday fact of life in South Africa, and the family and friends I visited were still fearful and distrustful of the newfound political stability. The country was still a simmering volcano.

My relationship with my father remained strained and distant, but his declining health—diabetes, heart disease, and peripheral neuropathy—had taken a toll. For once, he didn't harass me about getting married, and he seemed, if not soft, then at least more soft-spoken. I told him about my work and my bypass surgery, and he just listened.

In the months following my surgery, my health scare had also led me to some realizations about my future. In particular, I was growing increasingly resigned to living out my life alone. I had dated a few women after Karen, but nothing clicked. I was popular around the hospital and had lots of opportunities for relationships—surgeons, it seems, have no problem attracting romantic attention—but I preferred to be on my own rather than commit to the wrong person. I had been burned badly by my experience with Karen, and I wasn't about to make that mistake again. So that was that.

And then I met my wife.

About a year after my surgery, my friend Paul Weinberg, an emergency room doctor, told me that he knew the perfect woman for me.

Her name was Debbie Haag, and she worked as an emergency room nurse in Fountain Valley. It had been my habit to walk through the ER on the way to my office so I could see if there were any cases requiring a cardiac surgeon. Naturally, I took the opportunity to check her out.

The first thing I noticed about her was that she was talkative. My God, she could talk, and talk, and talk. But I liked that about her, appreciated that she was so animated and would speak up for herself. I also noticed that if something needed to be done for a patient, she acted immediately, decisively, and with compassion. I liked that too. The last thing I wanted was a meek, submissive partner, one reason Western women had always attracted me—their strength and assertiveness contrasted with the traditional Indian girls that my father wanted me to marry.

Debbie was nineteen years my junior and my opposite in many ways, from her gregarious personality to her middle-class Methodist upbringing in suburban Southern California. Yet I didn't notice the age difference, and I appreciated all the ways in which she was different from me. If anything, I felt that she made me young again; her natural vivaciousness cracked me out of my shell. On our first date, I showed up for dinner wearing polyester pants and a Hawaiian shirt. After that, she took me shopping to smarten my look. We quickly became inseparable, and every day was like a new adventure as I tried things I'd never even considered before. For the first time in my life, I slept in a tent on a camping trip and went rafting down river rapids, went kayaking and snowmobiling—we went to London, Kenya, and the Seychelles together. When I traveled to a medical exchange in Vietnam, Singapore, Hong Kong, and Malaysia, she tagged along. It was on that trip that we met Henry Heimlich, who, in

1974, had created the famous maneuver for dislodging objects from the airways of choking people.

It might sound corny, but when I was with Debbie, I felt truly alive.

When I started dating Debbie, my sister Padma and her family were still living with me, a detail that I had neglected to mention to Debbie. One day when she called the house, Padma answered the phone, and Debbie had a moment's panic that I was married. When I explained the situation, we had a good laugh, and I liked her even more. In the early days, Debbie was hesitant to flaunt our relationship in front of Padma and her family, so she would enter my house quietly through the back door and make a quick exit before everyone else woke up in the morning. We laughed about that too.

If my relationship with Debbie was an awakening, I soon discovered that I was overdue for another wake-up call.

My intense—some might say obsessive—perfectionism was having a negative effect on my colleagues. I had always prided myself on my exacting standards, which I saw as something I owed to my patients and as the only way to compete in the cutthroat world of cardiac surgery. That was why I was always on time, always available, and always willing to go to extra lengths to ensure that my patients received the very best. I was extremely diligent about postoperative care, and I never disappeared to let someone else deal with potential problems. The cardiologists I worked with appreciated that about me, because if one of their procedures went wrong, they would need a surgeon around to correct the problem. My growing practice and demanding workload led me to perform surgeries at hospitals throughout the county, yet I always made sure I was available whenever and wherever I was needed.

I had also prided myself on the steely composure that I had worked so hard to maintain. Even so, I must admit that there were times in the OR when that calm facade crumbled. Time is critical during heart surgery, and mistakes can be fatal. If there was a lapse—say, a nurse didn't have the correct size valve in the midst of a difficult procedure—I would sometimes blow up, shouting that, Goddamnit, that's unacceptable. These weren't my finest moments, but I rationalized to myself that I was the one ultimately responsible for the outcome of the surgery, and it was up to me to let those assisting me know when they had messed up.

Debbie had caught wind of some of the complaints about my behavior and urged me to ease up a little on the nurses, some of whom had become intimidated by me. But I didn't fully understand the depth of the problem until the hospital's executive board insisted that I seek treatment for my anger issues.

I was a little resentful at first. Didn't they understand the pressure I was under, and the stakes involved? How could they fault me for having high expectations? But after I began a series of sessions with a psychologist, my attitude began to change. He was sympathetic about the burdens of surgery, and he also empathized with me over my troubled background. For the first time, I started to recognize my anger and see that neither my lifelong habit of stifling my emotions nor my occasional outbursts in the OR were doing me or anyone else any good. Rather than barking at others who made mistakes and creating more tension in an already tense environment, I resolved to soften my tone and offer gentle corrections. I can't say that I was always successful, but at least I was more aware, and I was trying, at long last, to understand and deal more positively with the anger that burned inside me.

nineteen

HAPPINESS

DEBBIE AND I HAD PLANNED to take a romantic trip to Italy in March 1994, and I put her on notice that she should expect a big question from me while we were away.

I brought the ring with me and carried it wherever we went, waiting for just the right opportunity. Then one day, while we were visiting the peaceful island of Torcello in the Venice lagoon, the perfect moment presented itself. It was a beautiful, warm day, filled with sunshine. We sat down to rest surrounded by trees and flowers. Nearby, a cat lapped milk from a bowl, reminding me of how much Debbie loved cats.

I asked, and this time I knew what the answer would be, because for the first time in my life, everything felt so right.

We decided on a September wedding.

In April, Padma and her family moved out of my house, and Debbie's cat moved in. We bought a puppy and an SUV and sent out wedding invitations.

About a month before the wedding, I commented to Debbie that she was more emotional than usual, and I wondered if her seesawing moods were a product of wedding stress. But there was another explanation.

At fifty-two, I was about to get married for the first time and become a father for the first time. And although I was thrilled about having a child, I was also nervous. I was, after all, a physician, and I knew all too well the myriad things that can go wrong. As an older father, I was of course concerned about genetic abnormalities, and all sorts of complications can beset pregnant women, from hypertension to a ruptured uterus.

But I had also learned throughout my career in medicine that worrying does no good. After all my years of pushing ever forward and never stopping for reflection, I wanted to slow down and enjoy this wonderful time. I let the happiness wash over me.

Two years after my heart surgery, Debbie and I were married on a boat in Newport Harbor in front of 120 guests. Debbie's parents and two sisters were there, as were Amrit, Padma, Hansa, and Anjuli and many of our friends and coworkers. I wore a black tuxedo, and Debbie was stunning in her off-the-shoulder, tea-length white dress. Only her family knew that she was pregnant.

It was a nondenominational ceremony officiated by a ship captain decked out in a white coat, black pants, and naval hat that made him look like a character on *The Love Boat*. He had plenty of sea-related analogies, including references to "steadying the ship" and "the storms and reefs of matrimony." Under a flower-strewn arch, Debbie and I pledged our love and devotion to each other, exchanged rings, and were declared husband and wife. I made a quick toast, during which I joked about Debbie's last-minute desire to skip the big wedding and elope, and I told her that I loved her tremendously.

Then the party got under way, and boy, was it a party. There was plenty of food and drink, and most of our guests imbibed liberally. One couple got caught smoking a joint, and the boat operators issued a stern warning that such activities could get them in big trouble. We all danced and laughed, and by the time everyone disembarked near midnight, only a few sober souls, mainly my family members and, naturally, Debbie, set foot on the dock.

I sent a copy of the wedding video to my father, who was, true to form, not happy with my choice of bride or my American-style wedding. I admit that my motives for wanting him to see it weren't particularly generous, and I didn't harbor any misguided hope that he'd have a change of heart about my marriage. I knew exactly how he would react. "Why aren't you marrying an Indian girl?" he had demanded to know when we spoke on the phone shortly before the wedding. I replied that I was my own man and I was marrying the woman I wanted. Predictably, the video only stoked his anger, and as usual, I was unmoved by his displeasure.

I took Debbie to Ireland for our honeymoon. It was the twentieth reunion of my medical school class, so Debbie got to meet many of my former classmates. I also introduced her to Ruth and Ivan, and I was happy to see the two women get along famously.

After we returned home, we started attending Lamaze classes, just as any expectant couple would. And when I saw an ultrasound image of our baby girl sucking her thumb—yes, we learned we were to have a daughter—I was fascinated and thrilled. She looked perfect.

At last, everything was falling into place.

The puppy we had added to our growing family, a golden retriever named Romeo, was now eight months old and turned out to have such bad hip problems that he needed surgery. Debbie, then eight months into a normal pregnancy, was on her way to pick him up when the car in front of her braked suddenly and she ran into it from behind. She called me right away, and I dropped everything and met her at the scene. I was concerned, but she seemed fine, so we went home.

That night Debbie started getting abdominal cramps. We rushed to the hospital where we both worked, and she was admitted so the staff could keep an eye on her and the baby. The contractions subsided slightly, but during the night, the fetal monitor showed the baby's heart rate decelerating. It returned to normal but in the morning slowed again. There was no choice at that point, and an emergency cesarean section was ordered.

Debbie seemed apprehensive as the anesthesia was administered, but I kept my trademark calm exterior and silently prayed that our baby would be healthy. Back in my days at medical school and during my internship, I had participated in some births and C-sections. This time all I could do was stand back and watch. The procedure went well, and I even got to cut the umbilical cord.

And there she was, my perfect little munchkin. I checked her fingers, ears, nose, and face, and everything was normal. There were no signs of jaundice or the respiratory problems that are common in premature babies. She was only about five pounds, but she had a shock of black spiky hair, and she cried lustily and moved her little arms and legs just as a healthy baby should. The moment when she was wrapped in a blanket and handed to me was magical, that much more so because I had spent so much of my life alone, not knowing if I would ever feel this kind of joy.

Debbie's parents showed up a while later, and the nurses on duty, who knew both of us well, would stop by to get a peek at our little girl. We were surrounded by friendship and warmth, and I was filled with contentment. Debbie had given me another gift, one that I appreciated beyond measure. She told me that I should be the one to choose our daughter's name because I had waited so long to have my own family. I decided on Olivia Kanta-Lynn Dajee. I chose Olivia just because I liked it and Kanta-Lynn in honor of my and Debbie's mothers.

Amrit and my sisters gave me grief over our daughter's Western first name, but I stayed firm. I thought it ridiculous to lend importance to such parochial customs. My wife was American, I was now American, and my daughter was American, and I intended for her to grow up to be a strong, confident woman like her mother.

A few hours after Olivia was born, I was back in the operating room working on a damaged heart. I had that switch in my head, and I just turned it—*click*—and focused on the job while Debbie and our tiny daughter rested in the maternity ward.

After a few days, we took our baby home, and I was very cognizant of the fact that my life would be forever changed. I was now responsible for two lives, and I was determined to do well by my family. I would be a hands-on dad, I vowed, and I would teach my daughter that she must always follow her dreams, and never, ever let anyone tell her she isn't good enough.

Some of the changes I had expected. Fatherhood now meant that our child would always come first and that I must schedule my demanding workload around her needs—and at least try to have more of a normal routine.

I learned all the basics—changing diapers, walking with a stroller, calming the baby when she cried, holding her while she napped on my chest. Sometimes on the weekends when Debbie was at work, I would visit the hospital with Olivia in her bassinet. Debbie would cry when she saw her and call out, "Oh my God, here's my baby!"

But some aspects of having a baby—at least an American baby—had been a complete mystery to me. There was so much paraphernalia, some things I never even knew existed, and Debbie insisted on having only the best. There were bottles, car seats, tiny baby shoes, caps, mobiles to hang from the ceiling, tons of toys, and so many dainty little clothes. I was amused to learn that we had to be color coordinated and buy items that fit with themes. We took thousands of photos. It was all novel to me, and I found it hilarious and wonderful.

We took Olivia everywhere with us. Her first trip on a plane was at eight months old, when we went on a Hawaiian vacation. I'll never forget a strange moment: when we were at the airport waiting for the flight home, an older man approached us, telling us how cute Olivia was; he handed me twenty dollars and said, "This is for the baby." I tried to give it back, but he refused to take it. I couldn't figure out if he thought we were poor or if he just loved babies.

Olivia was a happy little girl, always smiling and friendly. When she was about three years old, she started in preschool, and I stayed sometimes to watch the kids play and chat with the other parents. It was like living a dream.

There was only one more thing we wanted to make our happiness complete: another child.

Himmet with his family in Newport Beach, California: wife Debbie, daughters Olivia and Isabelle, and dog Zane.

This time around, we were much more calm, and Debbie's second pregnancy was routine. In 1998, three and a half years after Olivia was born, we welcomed our second daughter into the world. This time it was Debbie's turn to pick the name, and she chose Isabelle Marie Dajee.

Our new baby girl was shy at first, but as they've grown older, my daughters have switched roles, and now Olivia is more reserved, while Isabelle is the social butterfly. But we've raised them both to be strong, work hard, and battle their way on their own—to get a good education and never be relegated to the kitchen to cook and clean for their husbands like obedient Indian girls. I tell them about South Africa, and how I had to fight for many of the things they take for granted. When we take them to traditional Indian events my family members host, I can see that they don't fit in, and though I tell them to be respectful, I'm quite glad that my girls are thoroughly American. That's just the way I wanted it.

twenty

LETTING GO

IN 1996, I'D HAD NEWS FROM SOUTH AFRICA. My father had been in declining health for some time. His heart disease and diabetes had worsened; his kidneys were failing; and my siblings and I were told that he had taken a sharp turn for the worse. Sharda asked Amrit and I what to do. Should he go on dialysis? After reviewing his condition, we saw no point in pursuing it and thought it kinder just to let him go peacefully. And that's exactly what happened. At the age of eighty-three, he slipped into a coma and never regained consciousness.

Though we had been quite distant for many years and resentment ran high on both sides, my father's passing gave me pause to reflect on his life and, yes, even to appreciate all that he had accomplished and what he had given to me.

I had to give the man credit. He came from nothing, had no formal education, and yet he traveled to a foreign land and scraped, fought, and sacrificed to create a better life for himself and his family. He built a business, kept expanding it, bought real estate, and through sheer force of will became a respected figure in our little Indian community. All of that took guts.

I had always attributed whatever success I'd achieved to my own perseverance, and to the support I'd received from my brothers and key friends, colleagues, and mentors along the way.

But when I look back, I realize that, crazy as I thought he was at times, my dad taught me many vital lessons—lessons that helped me throughout my life, including the importance of promptness, honesty, and respect for others. Though we disagreed, often bitterly, about the direction my life had taken, and about my refusal to adhere to tradition, he never wavered from his conviction that his children must be educated, and the value of that gift cannot be underestimated. My interest in politics and history also came from him; he taught me to be an avid reader and always to be interested in what was going on in the world. These are qualities I hope I've passed on to my own children.

And if I'm being fair, I probably got my stubbornness from him too. Like me, he believed that if you work hard and put your heart and soul into achieving your goals, never giving up, then you could have a better life.

Sometimes Amrit and I would reminisce about the old days and all that our father had achieved, and it was then that I would realize how remarkable he really was. Now that he was gone, it was time for me to let go of my anger. I had never been the son that my father had wanted me to be, but I had done well for myself and I was happy. And that was in no small part because of the start in life that he had given me.

Not long after he died, when Olivia was still a toddler and Isabelle not yet born, my father's widow, Sharda, traveled to California. She stayed with Amrit for a few days, and with some reluctance, I agreed to let her stay at my home for a few days as well. I was glad that I was busy at the hospital every day so I could avoid any confrontations or uncomfortable feelings. Debbie generously agreed to drive her around, taking her shopping and out to eat. It was a short visit and did nothing to bridge the icy divide that had always separated us.

The years after my daughters were born were the best of my life. I had everything I had always wanted—a successful surgical practice and a wonderful family of my own. Amrit and I were a team, and I was able to see my sisters regularly.

I still kept crazy hours, but that never bothered me. I was putting in about ten hours a day, six or seven days a week, performing two or three surgeries a day. Contracts with several HMOs guaranteed a steady stream of patients. I left home each morning before breakfast, grabbing meals on the go as I juggled work at several hospitals, mostly operating on hearts but also performing vascular, thoracic, and chest surgeries. My meticulous pre-op and post-op routines, teaching, seminars, and conferences were all still part of my normal work life, as were frequent middle-of-the-night emergencies. It's hard to believe that I could fit so much into each day, but somehow I did. When I look back, I think I must have been a maniac.

Amazingly, I never felt cheated out of time with my family, and for that I have Debbie to thank. She always kept me on track, made all our family plans and appointments, and let me know where I needed to be and when. If I got an urgent call, she always understood and urged me to go, saying that a patient's life might be at stake. Somehow I still made it to Christmas recitals and soccer and tennis games, usually taking a separate car just in case I had to leave on a moment's notice. We took Olivia and Isabelle everywhere—trips to Yellowstone and Hawai'i, skiing in Oregon, and annual vacations with two other families at a ranch in central California. I even sometimes took the girls with me when I did weekend hospital rounds. While I worked, they would wait in the doctors' lounge and eat in the cafeteria. They also liked to hang out at the nursing station, where they would draw pictures and the nurses would fuss over them. "Daddy, why does everybody say hi to you?" my girls once asked, to which I replied, "Because they know me."

The hardest part was holidays, when I would inevitably be called in for one reason or another. Thank God I had an understanding wife, for I wouldn't deny a patient if I thought I could make a difference. I never once asked about insurance; I took everyone, no questions asked, whether the patient was uninsured, unemployed, black, white, brown, young, or old. None of that mattered to me. If I could help, I would. When other doctors or nurses asked me to operate on their loved ones, I knew I had earned their confidence and respect, and that meant the world to me.

It should have come as no surprise, then, that nearly a decade after my bypass surgery, my heart rebelled again. The chest pain returned in the middle of the night, the same as before, about a three to four on a ten-point scale, spreading up to my jaw and down my left arm.

This time the images revealed a complete blockage in the left anterior descending artery—the widowmaker again—at the spot where it splits with a diagonal artery. The LAD feeds blood to the apex of the heart, while the diagonal branch supplies the heart muscle on the left side. The only reason I hadn't dropped dead from a heart attack or other major cardiac event was that the blood flow to the diagonal not only supplied that branch, as intended, but had also made a U-turn to flow back into the LAD. My body had forged its own impromptu bypass, like a traffic cop keeping cars moving around an accident site by diverting them into a lane normally used for opposing traffic.

I had cheated death once more, but this time it was entirely possible that my lifestyle had saved me. Yes, my work was still ridiculously stressful, and chronic stress contributes to the progression of heart disease, but since my first bypass surgery, I had made it a point to eat healthier meals and exercise regularly. Perhaps most important, though, was that I was truly happy, happier than I had ever been. I had a smart, strong wife who supported and looked after me and children who filled me with joy. Every time I went to a school function or a sporting event, or even just out to dinner with my family, I felt as though I were taking a mini-vacation from my surgical practice. It was as if all that happiness and fulfillment I was experiencing had gone to battle with my stress and genetics, and won. My heart had found its own way to keep ticking.

My medicines were adjusted again, essentially by cranking them up to full throttle, and the pains abated. I also resolved to reduce my frenetic workload to a more reasonable level. And I did reduce it for a while, but gradually I inched back up to my old routine. It was tough to say no; whenever I was asked to perform a surgery, I considered it my duty to oblige. Some people might say I was stupid for not cutting way back, but I didn't see it that way. I was like a poker player who knew and accepted the risks, and stuck with my bet that the hand I was dealt wouldn't let me down.

Over the years, I brought in a few partners to help with the workload, but except for Amrit, they usually only lasted a few years.

In many respects, my partnership with Amrit was a perfect match. He was an excellent surgeon, and as our practice continued to thrive I found myself relying on him heavily to assist me in the huge volume of cardiac cases I took on, and to take the lead on many of the thoracic surgeries that came our way. Because he was not board certified, the hospitals where we worked didn't want him to be the lead surgeon on cardiac cases. I asked him once what he thought the problem was and why he had never passed the certification exams, for he was obviously immensely skilled and should have qualified easily. He said that he didn't know; he'd studied, but he just couldn't pass. It was a feeling I knew well.

I think it upset Amrit greatly. He was still making a very good living, and he had plenty of work. But all the disappointments he'd encountered in his career must have been tough on him. Amrit, after all, had been the genius, the shooting star on whom so many expectations of greatness had been placed. He was doubly qualified, since he'd trained as a cardiac surgeon first in Britain and then again in the United States. But as time went on, he grew increasingly burned out and bitter because of all the politics, personalities, and bureaucratic nonsense within the medical establishment.

I was greatly indebted to Amrit for all that he had done for me, and I had thought to repay his support by giving him a place to go after he failed to earn tenure at UC Davis. But I saw how difficult it was for him to continue to play the game.

He never said anything, but I could sense the underlying tension, and it bothered me. Debbie and I would invite Amrit and his family over to our house, but as time went on, they stopped coming. Though we saw each other nearly every day at work, there was a growing distance between us.

In February 2005, I was attending a conference in Palm Springs when another physician approached me.

"How is your brother doing?" he asked. When I looked at him quizzically, he said, "Don't you know he had surgery yesterday?"

"What do you mean? Where?"

"At USC."

I was dumbstruck. Amrit had never said a word.

I rushed to my car and headed west. On the way, I called my sisters. Amrit had called Hansa, very likely after he'd already been admitted at the hospital, but inexplicably, he hadn't told her where he was or what was going on. When she asked where he was calling from, his reply was mysterious: "Far away," he said. I stopped at home to pick up Debbie, and we planned to meet my sisters and their husbands at USC. Rain fell as we drove north.

I later learned that Amrit had become short of breath, a sign of heart failure, and had gone to the UC Irvine Medical Center, near where we lived. But the doctors at UCI decided that his condition was so severe and complex that he should be transferred to USC, which had a more advanced cardiac surgical unit. He was taken there by ambulance.

By the time I arrived, the situation was grim. Amrit had already undergone coronary bypass and mitral valve replacement surgery. He was on a ventilator and had an assist device supporting his left heart. The surgery had been critical, and he wasn't recovering as hoped. The heart muscle had simply been too damaged. I wondered if he could have been a transplant candidate before they rushed to try to repair his heart, but the question was now moot—whatever window there might have been had closed. Despite the surgical team's best efforts, Amrit was dying.

He was still conscious when I first saw him, but he was intubated and couldn't speak. I leaned over and spoke softly. "Don't worry," I told him. "They said the surgery was fine and you're going to do well." He nodded, but I'll never know whether he fell for my lie.

He lingered for twelve days. His right heart began to fail too, and he was taken off of all assist devices and medications. There was no point. Soon, his heart stopped for good. He was seventy years old.

For the second time, I had lost a brother and I couldn't understand why. I sat down at home one night shortly afterward to think about how Amrit had died. I couldn't make sense of it, and the feeling of futility tortured me. He hadn't called me, hadn't sought my advice or help. I could have taken him to UCLA, where I had contacts and could have made certain that he received the best possible care from surgeons I knew and trusted. That kind of thing can help.

Instead, he had shut me out, had not even shared with me that he was sick. It's true that we'd had a complicated, sometimes enigmatic relationship, but for him to hide his condition from me seemed completely out of character. He'd been so smart. How could he be so foolish? Why hadn't he trusted me? Why?

I wondered if he'd known that he was dying and that any measures would only have delayed the inevitable. I wasn't involved in his treatment and didn't see his records, so I don't know if another course of action could have made a difference. Perhaps he simply chose to let go.

I thought of a patient on whom I had once operated. Over the years, through thousands of interactions with patients and their families, I had learned to deliver the unvarnished truth about the chances of a successful surgery, discuss the options thoroughly, let the patient think it through, and never push. If I pressured a patient into a high-risk surgery and he died, I'd have to live with that. This particular patient, I remembered, was a guy in his fifties and a risky case, but I said that I'd give surgery a shot if that was what he wanted. He decided to go ahead and take the chance. I did everything I could possibly do, but he died within a day after the surgery.

Afterward, my secretary told me that the patient's wife wanted to speak with me. I braced myself; sometimes people just look for someone to blame. As it turned out, she wasn't angry. She just wanted to talk. She told me that she had insisted that her husband have the surgery and that he had told her that he knew he'd never wake up from it. That kind of thing stays with you.

Perhaps Amrit had known his fate too. But for the rest of my life, I'll never know what was going on in his head. It's a puzzle I'll never solve, a question that will forever haunt me.

My last days with Amrit are just bitter memories now.

That summer I went back to South Africa, this time with Debbie and the girls. Amrit's death, and my own heart condition, weighed heavily on my mind. I wanted to pay a visit to my remaining family and friends. And I wanted to show my wife and daughters where I came from, to help them understand that part of me.

Much of the trip was devoted to playing tourist. We went on a safari, staying in luxurious tents at the Mala Mala Game Reserve in Kruger National Park, where we saw water buffaloes, rhinos, elephants, zebras, giraffes, and many other wild animals. At night, we could see their eyes illuminated in the darkness, and it seemed as if they were staring straight at us. The girls were shocked when we saw four lions tear apart and devour a pregnant gazelle, and I had to explain to them that nature could be brutal and that the stronger animals survive by eating the weaker ones.

In Cape Town, we went to see the penguins at Simons Town and the baboons at Cape Point. At a monkey park midway between Cape Town and Port Elizabeth, Olivia burst into tears when a monkey stole her "I Love New York" bracelet. We visited UCT, Table Mountain, and Robben Island, where Mandela and many other political prisoners had been held, and were led on a tour by a former inmate. I took my family to the District 6 Museum, near my old home, so they could learn about the savagery of apartheid.

We spent time with Dhiraj and Belle and their three grown children in Johannesburg, to which they had relocated many years before, and with my half brother Naresh, and we traveled to Cape Town to visit my cousins and old friends. Everyone was shocked and devastated by Amrit's death. My big brother, the

Himmet in South Africa, with Table Mountain in the background.

first in our small Indian community to become a cardiac surgeon, had been revered among our kind. That he'd succumbed to heart disease himself seemed almost unthinkable. They were all working through their grief and struggling to understand how it could have happened to him, of all people.

On all my previous trips to South Africa, as soon as I landed, I couldn't wait to leave. This time was different, because Debbie and the girls were with me, and they were thoroughly enjoying themselves. We spent a leisurely two and a half weeks, and I found myself, if not excited, at least somewhat hopeful because of all the changes I witnessed. Mandela, by then retired from the presidency, was still a powerful presence. There were no more "Whites Only" signs. I could go anywhere without being harassed. Indeed, I could walk down the street side by side with my wife, who is white, and no one could stop me. Everywhere we went, I shook my head in astonishment.

Yet I still wasn't convinced that it would last, and fears over the high crime rate and continuing bloodshed still ran high among my friends and family. In 2003, Dhiraj had been twice held up at gunpoint in his pharmacy. The first time, four intruders barged in together. Two of them pinned him against some shelves, holding their guns to his chest, while the other two emptied his till. The second incident occurred eight months later, when three armed men burst in and demanded his car keys and cash. One of them ordered Dhiraj and two employees to the back of the store at gunpoint and told them to lie face down. My brother was certain it was all over for him, but the thieves let them be. After that, Dhiraj, at his children's urging, gave up and liquidated his business.

His weren't the only disturbing stories I heard. One Indian man I had known from the old community had been beaten up by thugs, and another acquaintance had been stabbed to death in Simon's Town. South Africa undoubtedly had a long way to go before it would be a secure and stable democracy.

In short, I was still skeptical about the détente with the Afrikaners. I didn't believe they would submit to the ideal of a society in which all races are free and equal. The threat of civil war still seemed very real to me.

twenty-one

COURAGEOUS HEART

THE YEAR AFTER MY TRIP TO SOUTH AFRICA with my family, the pains in my chest paid me another unwelcome visit, awakening me once again in the middle of the night.

It had been fifteen years since my bypass surgery, and although I had improved my diet, exercised regularly, and took my medicine religiously, my healthy lifestyle had succeeded only in slowing, not stopping, the progression of the disease. Images showed that the atherosclerosis, or plaque buildup, had reappeared in my arteries and was now in the vein grafts that had been put in during the surgery. Luckily, I'd never had a heart attack, but the recurring chest pain was a constant warning bell that more intervention was needed. I saw Dr. Laks again, and we decided that a second round of bypass surgery was my best option. He agreed to do the surgery.

Redoing a bypass offers no guarantees. In fact, these types of surgeries can be exceedingly difficult. I should know; I'd done plenty of them myself. Often the surgeon must peel away layers of dense scar tissue from the previous surgery. There's a risk of massive bleeding and of dislodging debris from the built-up plaque, which can then migrate, causing a heart attack or stroke. And the images taken beforehand can tell the surgeon only so much about what awaits inside, which means a lot of quick, on-your-feet improvisation. Generally, a second go-round on a bypass is a longer, more complicated operation, the surgical equivalent of dancing through a minefield. My case was no exception.

During the procedure, my internal body temperature was lowered to twenty-four degrees to slow my metabolism, and Dr. Laks found plenty of challenges awaiting him inside my heart. He used a radial artery from an arm to bypass my LAD, but he wasn't able to salvage my internal mammary artery from the first surgery and had to use a vein graft. The diagonal artery that had saved me after my previous bypass was now diseased throughout its length, a development that hadn't shown up on the angiogram. My right ventricle was bulging due to ischemia, or reduced blood flow, and Dr. Laks had to do some fast thinking to get around the distended area. All told, it was a highly technical procedure requiring immense skill and creativity to navigate around all the blocked passageways and narrowed thoroughfares of my heart. Thank God I was in expert hands.

Afterward, my blood was rewarmed and I was slowly weaned off the heart-lung machine. When I awoke, I had tubes in my nose and throat, but once they were removed, I felt much better. I looked to see if there was an intra-aortic balloon pump to support my heart, which would have told me that something had gone wrong during the surgery. There was none, and I felt instantly relieved. Still, when Debbie brought Olivia and Isabelle to visit, the girls, just eleven and eight years old at the time, must have been a little bewildered when they saw me lying there with all those lines sticking out of me and attached to various gizmos.

My recovery was nothing short of remarkable. My blood flow was excellent. I was up and walking the next day and discharged after about five days. Once again, I was a lucky man.

But when I returned home, I knew that I had to face reality. After caring for thousands of patients over the years, it was time for me to take care of myself. My practice was still thriving; I was in greater demand than ever, and my skills were as sharp as they had ever been. The thought of giving it all up made me sad, especially after all the battles I had fought and all the years of training I had endured to earn my place in a very selective profession. Sometimes I would run into former patients in the hospital pharmacy, or when I was out and about, shopping at a mall, buying groceries, or even at parties. Without fail, they would thank me profusely. Whenever that happened, I knew that it had all been worth it. Yet returning to the enormous stress of cardiac surgery could have cost me my life. I had accomplished everything I had wanted in my career and had pushed myself as far as my heart could take it. My wife and kids had given me something else to live for. Now I wanted more than anything to see my girls grow up.

While I gave the matter some serious consideration, and I discussed it with Debbie, I didn't agonize. I had lived my life so far moving always to the future, never obsessing over what could have been, and that philosophy had worked well for me. So when I decided that I had operated on my last heart, I did it quickly and without regret. No looking back.

By that time, Debbie had also retired from nursing, another decision that physical considerations had forced upon us. After the girls were born, she had cut back on her hours, but she loved nursing and had continued working about four shifts a month on a per diem basis. But two years before my second bypass surgery, Debbie had taken a nasty spill while trying to get our dogs indoors on a rainy night. She hit the ground hard, landing face down in the mud, and her ankle turned sideways as it snapped in half. It was the worst possible way to break an ankle.

The next morning, she had surgery to put in plates and screws to secure the shattered bones. It was a long time before she could put any weight on that leg, and she had to suffer through several more surgeries and many months of painful physical therapy. Debbie wasn't happy about it, but her nursing career was over. Long shifts, with all the standing and walking required, were out of the question.

Now I would be joining my wife in retirement. It took me a couple months to wind down my practice. I had to clear out my office, inform all the professional societies of my status, and break the news to the hospitals and cardiologists who had relied on my services.

If I had continued on with my surgical practice, I would have faced a rapidly changing landscape. The trend for some time had been for cardiologists to take on more and more of the less invasive procedures, such as angioplasties and stent insertions. That shift has only increased in the years since, as more percutaneous approaches—approaches through the skin—have increasingly replaced many of the major surgical interventions that were common during my career. These new technologies have resulted in a declining volume of work for heart surgeons, but they have also meant that surgeons are getting called in for the more difficult, highest-risk cases, or ones in which the cardiologists find complications setting in after their procedures. This has made for a tricky business, because surgeons' mortality and morbidity rates are made public. My rates were always good, but it's probably no coincidence that in recent years, fewer physicians have been choosing to pursue cardiac surgery. Why would they invest in the long years of training when they were destined to receive only high-risk cases with a low rate of success?

Yet some of the advancements in the field have been truly amazing. Robotics, genetics, 3D printing, stem cell technology— these are the future. Today, replacement valves are successfully grown in labs; at some point, we'll see entire lab-grown hearts. People will look back on open-heart surgery and say, "You mean you used to crack open patients' chests and cut up their hearts? How barbaric!" I don't mind that my old job is destined to become obsolete. The less invasive, the better. That's progress. I'm just grateful that I'm still around to bear witness to so many wonderful developments.

In late 2006, at the age of sixty-four, I left it to younger generations to carry the torch.

I've always lived my life with purpose, relentlessly moving forward, never looking back. Someone might ask why I didn't stay in South Africa, or return there after medical school, and fight for change. It's a fair question. All I can say is that we all have our own paths to take. I believe that the one I chose was the right one for me, and I hope I've helped some people along the way. I have no regrets over the choices I've made, and if I had to do it all again, I know without hesitation that I'd do everything exactly the same way.

But living without regret doesn't mean I don't still have empty places in my heart. I've never been one to put my emotions on display; instead, I've kept them buried deep, hidden away as the years have gone by. Yet they are still there. The anguish over the loss of the two people who mattered most to me, until I met Debbie and became a father, has never gone away. That sadness will always live inside of me.

I wish that my mom could have known my wife and kids. When she died, it was as if the bottom fell out of my life. She was my source of solace and comfort, and though we all picked up the pieces and did the best we could, nothing was ever the same. She was so soft and sweet, and though she had been very much a traditional Indian woman, I believe she would have opened her heart and embraced my American wife and daughters.

Bhanu, I have no doubt, would have loved them unreservedly. He would have appreciated Debbie's boisterous personality and generous spirit, and he would have lavished attention on my girls, bouncing them on his knee, bringing them gifts, and telling stories to delight them. I think he would have been proud of all my accomplishments. I am well aware that he made a large part of my journey possible, yet if he were here today, he would take no credit for all the many ways he helped me and stood by me when no one else believed I was worthy.

My mind often wanders to thoughts of Bhanu at the strangest times. Like when I'm loading dishes in the dishwasher and it sets me reminiscing about the days sitting around his kitchen table dreaming up our fanciful ideas for business ventures, some of which, like for prepackaged laundry detergent, were ahead of their time. I don't give over to melancholy, but I grow quiet in these moments and think, *If only.* Yet I feel he is here with me;

his spirit still follows me and guides me when I need him most. He was standing beside me at my wedding, and he shared in my joy when my children were born. Every time I set foot in an operating room, he held my hands steady and reminded me that I could accomplish the impossible. I made broken hearts beat again because he told me I could do it.

All my life, I've known adversity and disappointment. I could fill a book with all the rejection letters I've received. But I worked every angle, cultivated connections, and never took no for a final answer. If someone says I've been lucky, I reply, that's true, but that most of the time, I had to make my own luck. My name means "courage." That's what I always told myself when times were tough and I began to despair. And it would be enough to keep me going, to persevere despite the odds.

My heart is strong. I am a man named Courage.

Epilogue

IN SPRING 2014, I BEGAN A JOURNEY.

For the first time in my life, I started to look back. Introspection has never come naturally to me, but I believed it was at last time for me to pause in my relentless march forward, to take stock of all the forces that had helped to shape me, and to reflect on how I came to earn the life I had so fervently desired.

My reason for doing so was simple enough. I wanted my daughters to understand all that I had endured, the obstacles I had encountered, and the challenges I had overcome, simply because I had refused to give up. I had watched as Olivia, by then a college student, and Isabelle, working her way through high school, had blossomed into the strong, independent young women I always wanted them to be. True, they've had many advantages in life, yet all people, no matter where they come from or how they are raised, are bound to suffer setbacks. I hoped to inspire my girls, through my story, to push away any doubts they might have about themselves and to pursue their goals with the same dogged tenacity that got me where I am. If other people feel touched by my story, so much the better.

I had for some time very much wanted to see Dhiraj again. I hadn't seen him since my visit with Debbie and the girls a decade earlier. We were both getting along in years, and Dhiraj and Belle had been dealing with health problems of their own. My brother

191

had recently undergone treatment for vocal cord cancer, and his raspy throat had made phone conversations difficult. Belle, meanwhile, suffered from chronic obstructive pulmonary disease.

But our reunion, in fall 2015, would also give me the opportunity to confront the past I had so diligently spurned for so long. I planned to go alone this time, to see relatives and old friends, to revisit my former homes and many of the places I had frequented when I was young, and to meet with some people who might help me with my research into my own past.

As I prepared to leave, I was struck by an entirely novel sensation, one I could hardly believe I was feeling: I was excited by the prospect of returning to South Africa.

I started near Johannesburg, in the suburb where Dhiraj and Belle have lived for many years, where many of the residents work in the aerospace industry and the streets, lined with beautiful old eucalyptus and jacaranda trees, have names like "Lockheed" and "Bombardier." It's a primarily white area where they wouldn't have been allowed to live during apartheid, but it is slowly becoming more racially mixed. My brother, still shy and quiet after all these years, picked me up from my hotel and took me to his home, where Belle and their three children—all now in their thirties and early forties—were waiting. We were joined by my half brother Naresh, who lived nearby in Pretoria and worked in information technology. It was a hot, dry day, and we sat in the garden and enjoyed a lovely sunset barbecue of lamb, pork, and chicken dishes, fragrant with the Indian spices I knew so well. I was happy to see that Dhiraj, who had finished his radiation treatments, appeared to have recovered well, and Belle seemed to have her COPD under control.

The next day, even hotter than the last, I traveled to Pretoria, the administrative capital of South Africa, with my brothers. I had lived in South Africa for twenty-seven years, but I had never before visited this seat of power. I had never wanted to go there; I had considered it an evil place where the architects of apartheid helped build the legal structures of institutionalized racism. But now I wanted to see it, if only to appreciate the fact that the Afrikaners no longer controlled the government. We walked around the stately government buildings and lush gardens and stopped before a huge bronze statue of Mandela, arms outstretched, that had been installed two years earlier. My brothers and I talked about how remarkable it was to see this awe-inspiring tribute to a man that the Afrikaners had once treated as a traitor.

We went to the Voortrekker Monument nearby, and the contrast could not have been more stark. The imposing monolith was built in 1949 to commemorate the Great Trek of the Boers—as the Afrikaner settlers were called—from the Cape into the northern interior, a journey that they undertook in the 1830s after the British had pissed them off by abolishing slavery. This towering symbol of apartheid has been rebranded in recent years as a more benign commemoration of Afrikaner history. As I gazed at the granite reliefs that depicted the supposedly heroic white settlers fighting off the savage natives, I had to hand it to them. The Afrikaners built the country on the backs of the blacks, pummeling the native tribes into submission, and then they had the temerity to build this magnificent structure to honor that subjugation. And I thought to myself, *The bastards*.

Later, I made another important stop in my journey. Opened in 2001, the Apartheid Museum in Johannesburg chronicles the history of the race-based system in all its wretchedness.

As I toured the museum, its many images rekindled my burning hatred: the signs I remembered so vividly from my youth, the ones designating areas and facilities that could only be used by whites; a placard with a quote from a House of Assembly debate in 1950: "The white man is the master in South Africa and the white man from the very nature of his origins, from the very nature of his birth, and the very nature of his guardianship, will remain master in South Africa to the end"; a photo of a poor black woman scrubbing toilets she wasn't allowed to use.

I met with Emilia Potenza, the museum's curator of exhibitions and education, who graciously agreed to accompany me around the facility and answer my questions. I had written to her before I left on the trip, telling her about Bhanu's story and asking if she might have any more information to give me. When I arrived, she showed me a list of casualties from the Soweto Uprising. More than one thousand names were on it, Bhanu's included. The documents she showed me said that he had been killed by gunshot to the chest by South African police "during the looting of a store."

"Bullshit," I told her.

She said that the museum was planning a new permanent exhibit on the uprising, which would include a placard containing the list of all the victims. Bhanu's name would be on it, she assured me. That gave me a small measure of comfort, and I promised that I would return to South Africa to see it.

Later, after I told Dhiraj and Belle what I had discovered, they told me a story that I had never heard before—a story about a shocking incident that occurred about six months after Bhanu's death.

Belle and Dhiraj had been in their home in Cape Town when suddenly a bullet tore through a window and lodged into the cushion of a sofa on which Belle was seated, very nearly hitting her. There was a knock on the door. Belle opened it and was faced with a police officer. He told her that the police had been chasing a criminal in the area. Seeing that a bullet had gone astray, he was checking to see if anyone was hurt. Poor Belle was terrified. She told the officer that she didn't want any trouble and that her brother-in-law had been shot to death on the streets of Retreat.

The cop's reply was stunning. He said he had been working in Retreat on the day that Bhanu died.

"That could have been me who shot him," he said.

There was so much looting and chaos in the area that day, he told her, that the police were firing pretty much indiscriminately into the crowd. He said he didn't know that a shopkeeper had been hit. "It could have been me. We were all shooting," he said.

Out of her mind with fear, Belle just wanted the guy to leave. He gave her his phone number in case she wanted to ask him any questions later, but she never called, and she didn't hear from him again.

Could the police really have mistaken Bhanu for a looter? It was difficult to believe. He had just gone down to the street, hoping to retrieve the shop keys from his car. Amrit had collected Bhanu's clothing from the morgue and had described the blood-soaked shirt, riddled with fifty or sixty pellet holes. That would indicate that Bhanu had been shot at a close range, because buckshot sprays when it is fired. It seemed to me that the police considered him a fair target only because he'd dared to go outside with the wrong skin color. That was not a mistake—it was a horrendous injustice, one of many the government perpetrated under the guise of law and order.

I spent three days in Johannesburg and then headed to Cape Town. At the airport, waiting to board the plane for the two-hour flight, I listened, fascinated, to a conversation between two men, one white, one black. They were sitting side by side, and the white guy was helping the black fellow figure something out on his smartphone. The black man held a science book, suggesting that he was well educated. The pair were laughing and chatting as if they were old friends, and I thought to myself that never in my life had I expected to see that in South Africa.

After my arrival in Cape Town, I checked into a room overlooking the marina in the elegant Cape Grace Hotel. The entire waterfront area was so different from my youthful memories. Remade for tourists, it was no longer the rough-and-tumble industrial working dock where my brothers and I used to talk our way onto the ships. Now it was lined with luxury hotels, restaurants, and shops, and I heard that an expansion was under way to add new cruise liner berths. I marveled at all these signs of upscale economic activity.

The plan was for Harsheila to pick me up and take me to her home for dinner. My half sister's life is another testament to change in South Africa. Harsheila and her husband have had successful careers, hers in corporate training and development and his in the food industry. They have a son in his twenties who earned an architecture degree from UCT and a daughter who had recently been accepted into the School of Medicine at Stellenbosch University—the same institution that wouldn't allow me to participate in an exchange program when I was in college.

I presented Harsheila with a bouquet of proteas, the colorful South African flowering plant also known as sugarbush. But before continuing on to her house, we had a stop to make, one that I had specifically requested.

We went to the home of my stepmother, Sharda, to pick her up and take her to dinner with us.

It might seem odd that I had wanted to see her after so many years and hurt feelings. But I had no desire to dig up old bones, nor did I want or expect any apologies. I simply decided that it was time to put any lingering resentment over her treatment of my siblings and me behind me. I would say hello, show her respect, and try to have a cordial conversation with her. That would be enough.

It was a chilly, windy day, so we stayed inside at Harsheila's impressive suburban home, a newly built, modern structure with an open floor plan and environmentally friendly features. We dined on spicy Indian soup, two kinds of fish, and vegetables.

When I first saw Sharda, we greeted each other with the traditional "namaste," and I gave her a hug, while I silently mused that it was probably the first time we had ever embraced. I could see that she was in agony from arthritis pain in her knee and shoulder. In her mid-eighties, she walked slowly and gingerly, leaning on a cane for support. She chatted about her health and then started reminiscing about my father.

In his last few years, my dad had suffered greatly from neuropathy and had begun to drink heavily, she said. He was a fighter to the last, she told me, and I thought to myself, *That son of a gun, that's him. He would never give up.*

Our conversation was polite but stilted and as chilly as the breezes blowing across the Cape. She asked me few questions, and I sensed no remorse in her. She must be miserable, I thought, living by herself with nothing but her memories and aching joints for company. Perhaps I could finally see her in a different light. She was reserved by nature and had been caught up in her own needs and desires, leaving little room to sympathize with the unruly characters that her demanding new husband had brought into her life. It had been painful for my brothers and sisters and me at the time, but that was long past. I don't know if she'd changed, but perhaps I had.

When I returned to my hotel that night, I felt that my animosity toward my stepmother could at last be put to rest.

South Africa is a strange country. It has three capitals: while the president and his cabinet are in Pretoria, Bloemfontein is the judicial capital, and Cape Town is home to the legislative branch.

In my youth, I had seen the graceful colonnaded colonial-era Parliament buildings in central Cape Town more times than I can count. The morning after my dinner at Harsheila's house, as a crisp spring breeze kept temperatures mild, I passed by once again, and by the sandstone facade of St. George's Cathedral, where, in 1989, the legendary Archbishop Desmond Tutu led more than thirty thousand people in a mass protest against apartheid.

I was headed to the South African Public Library, located in a neoclassical building with Corinthian columns at the corner of Wale Street and Victoria, in the beautiful, lush gardens where I had spent many days when I was young. I wanted to visit the library to look up old news clippings from around the time of Bhanu's death, to refresh my memory about what else had been going on in the world, and to see what the South African press had been reporting.

I learned that Mao Zedong, chairman of the Communist Party in China, had died on the same day as my brother, September 8, 1976. In that same month, Samora Machel, the president of Mozambique and an anti-apartheid sympathizer, had perished in a plane crash; rumor had it that the South African government was responsible. In New York's Yankee Stadium, world heavyweight champion Mohammed Ali, who was idolized by black South Africans, fought Ken Norton. Ali won in a highly controversial decision.

I continued to flip through articles from the South African papers. One quoted a government minister who blamed the "skollies"—a South African slang word for gangsters or ruffians—for all the violence. In another, South African prime minister B. J. Vorster downplayed the government's response, asserting that only limited force had been employed to establish order. That month, U.S. secretary of state Henry Kissinger had one of a series of meetings with Vorster to negotiate a path for the future of South Africa and neighboring countries.

I came across a story in the *Cape Times,* published on September 9, the day after Bhanu's shooting, that referred to the riot police using buckshot.

Nowhere was there mention of any innocent lives cut short by that buckshot.

And then I found, printed in the *Cape Argus* newspaper, also on September 9, this tribute submitted by Dhiraj and Belle:

> Bhanudey passed away tragically Wednesday 8. He had a heart purer than gold and to those who loved him his memory will never grow old.

I allowed a thought I had avoided for nearly four decades finally to surface. If I had been there, in South Africa, could it have turned out differently? If we'd been together, would Bhanu still be alive?

When I saw Trafalgar, my former high school, I was struck by how small it was, just a single building; yet it was a remarkable institution that had produced so many talented people. I strolled along the familiar corridors with their whitewashed walls and checked out the big assembly hall where we would take our exams. A photograph of Basil February, the slain civil rights activist, hung on one wall. I poked my head inside some of the classrooms. A conference room was dedicated to Dullah Omar, a onetime Trafalgar student who became minister of justice under President Mandela.

The next day, I went to the District 6 Museum and wandered through the exhibits. Again I saw the old signs and placards that enforced racial separation. One display showed how many nonwhites had lived, with eight or ten people crammed into one room. I saw an old typewriter like the one my family used to own and another exhibit on the forced removals of nonwhites from their homes. There was a bench marked "Europeans Only," and seeing that made my blood boil. "Let me sit on this goddamned thing," I said, and I did. I even got my mixed-race driver to join me.

As we left the museum, I noticed the big brick police head-quarters building across the street, and my mind wandered back to the day that Dhiraj and I joined with our Trafalgar teachers and classmates to march there to protest the Sharpeville Massacre. The multicolored South African flag, adopted in 1994 to represent diversity, flapped on a flagpole out front, and all the police officers I saw entering and exiting the building were nonwhite. This place, which had once represented everything I had hated, was now just another building.

It was much the same at the site of my family's old home and shoe shop on Sir Lowry Road. Not even our old number, 125, remained. Now a big tire store inhabits the space where our shop and all the neighboring shops once stood. I walked around the corner and knocked on the door of a small house. A woman answered, and when I told her who I was, she said she remembered my father and asked after my sisters; she remembered them playing in the street when they were young.

The bus depot next to the building where Bhanu's restaurant had been was still there, but a different company was running it. The restaurant itself was long gone, and the building was unrecognizable; it had either been thoroughly renovated or knocked down and rebuilt. It was disappointing, to be honest. I know that things change. But I was looking for some trace of nostalgia, a remnant of a memory, and there was none. It was as if someone had taken a cloth and wiped away a piece of my life.

Site of the family's shoe store in Cape Town, now occupied by a tire store.

I signed up for a tour of UCT's medical school at Groote Schuur Hospital, where Christiaan Barnard and his brother Marius performed the first successful human heart transplant in December 1967. Inside the hospital is the Heart of Cape Town Museum, which I had very much wanted to see. It contains many artifacts, exhibits, and painstaking re-creations of the historic transplant operation. I saw Dr. Barnard's dog lab, where he and his team experimented on canines, and operating rooms with wax sculptures of Barnard and his assisting physicians and nurses. It was fascinating, but also a bit eerie.

At the Cape Grace Hotel, I met with the then deputy vice-chancellor of UCT Anwar Mall, who is also of Indian descent. Through the kindness of his friend and colleague Professor Howard Phillips, Dr. Mall helped me get ahold of my old UCT records, including all my applications and the documents showing that I had received government permission to attend. (I had been required to reapply every year.) One document showed that my medical school application had been given the green light by the government, but it was UCT that had turned me down.

There was one surprise in the paperwork, a letter from the dean who had called me into his office to ask how I had managed to get into UCT as an undergraduate. I'd assumed he had helped to close the loophole through which I'd slipped, but I'd been wrong; the letter showed that he'd been sympathetic to nonwhites and had been trying to work the system to secure admission for another Indian student. This was no small thing, for by doing so, he was putting his own career on the line.

I had jumped to an incorrect conclusion about the dean because of the way so many other white people had treated nonwhites. Amrit too had faced continual roadblocks during his years at UCT. It was a big deal in our community when he gained acceptance to the prestigious medical school, as he was only the second person we knew who had made it that far. Yet even though the school had let him in, it really hadn't let him in all the way. He was never allowed to examine white patients. He couldn't even lay a finger on the white flesh of a body that was beyond the point of caring as it lay cold and dead awaiting dissection in anatomy class.

I had faced this kind of racism every step of the way as I fought for my own right to be educated. Yet after seeing the dean's letter, I felt guilty for having assumed the worst about him. The picture I'd constructed out of anger and mistrust had actually been more complicated than I'd realized. I was reminded yet again that many whites in South Africa had been fervently opposed to apartheid, and some had risked their careers, relationships, and possibly even their lives to extend a helping hand to nonwhites like me.

After UCT, I went to visit my old friend Reg Muller, the boatbuilder who had employed me as I awaited my departure for Ireland. Over the years, we had kept in touch through phone calls and e-mails, but I hadn't seen him since I left for medical school in 1969. At ninety, Reg still looked sturdy and healthy, and we engaged in a lively discussion about politics, books, philosophy, and emerging technologies such as robotics. I asked him why he, a white man, had taken a chance on hiring me to help him build his boat. He said he could sense how driven I was and that he believed I would be a success one day. I was glad I had the opportunity to thank him for encouraging me to keep reaching for more.

It took me a few days to work up the nerve to make the one stop on my journey that I knew I must face. But finally I asked my amiable driver to take me to Retreat, to the place where Bhanu had died.

It was all so different from my memories. The building where Bhanu's clothing store had been located had long ago been torn down; there was nothing there now but an empty lot. Across the street had been a grocery store and pharmacy; the buildings were still there, but many of the shops had changed. On the next block over, I saw a doctor's office and went inside. The doctor, who looked to be a few years older than me, said he had been there that day during the rioting and had also closed early. He'd heard that Bhanu had been shot, but he'd been too afraid to venture outside.

I stood alone in the quiet road and tried to imagine what it must have been like: the pandemonium as the crowds surged down the street, chased by riot police; Bhanu caught up in the bedlam, torn between terror and worry over the damage to his store.

My mind wandered to happier times. I thought of all the times I had spent in that shop, working at the counter, shooting the breeze with my brother, telling jokes, chatting about our lives and all our hopes and dreams. I used to love going there. He had a way of talking, of cajoling customers, but not in a manipulative way. He genuinely liked people, and he was generous to a fault, always the guy who would make people smile and feel at home. No one ever had a bad word to say about Bhanu.

I remembered the books with political themes—about two hundred books in all—each one banned by the government,

Corner where Bhanu's clothing store once stood. The building is long gone; all that remains is an empty lot. He was gunned down by police nearby during the Soweto Uprising in 1976.

that we had hidden in the crawl space above the ceiling. We had burned them in a bonfire for fear they'd be discovered. I had been so angry back then, so consumed by my burning ambition to get the hell out of South Africa. Looking back at those precious memories, it was as if I were gazing at a painting I had walked past a thousand times, but only now could I fully understand its true value.

I couldn't find the exact spot where he had been shot. It was somewhere on that street corner—that was all I knew. I felt the bile rise up again, dark and bitter. So many people, so many families, had been destroyed by apartheid. And for what? So the white man could call himself master? Bhanu had been the best of the best, the purest soul and kindest heart, and he'd been killed for nothing. Even after all this time, I couldn't come to grips with it, couldn't fathom the loss of this magnificent human being. How I wished that his store would appear and I could walk in and talk to him as I had in the old days. I imagined how it could have been. He could have adopted children and moved to the United States where we would have all lived side by side. We could have grown old together. As I lingered, yearning for the impossible, I searched for some sense of his spirit, a whisper or a shadow. But it wasn't there, not in this place. All I could feel was that familiar harsh, aching sorrow.

I had come to South Africa to confront my past, but when it came to revisiting my brother's death, there could be no resolution. I have never given in to despair, have refused to let his death destroy me too. But there will never be closure. As I stood on the street where his life ended, I knew this truth more than ever.

When the time came for me to journey back to California, I felt strangely reluctant to leave. I had been so happy to spend time with family, particularly Dhiraj, and I had learned so much. Yet, as I prepared to go, I had the feeling that I'd left much unfinished business: questions that had led to more questions, and a never-to-be-satisfied longing for what was, or what might have been. Perhaps I'll return again soon, I told Dhiraj, and said my good-byes.

I have no illusions about the changes that I witnessed. My former country is one of the most beautiful places on earth, but the South Africa that most tourists see isn't the real one—not the one I know, at any rate. Even now, it is only what can charitably be described as a work in progress. More than two decades after the fall of apartheid, many deeply entrenched problems remain, and much of the hope that Mandela had inspired through his courage and commitment to a better future had been faltering badly, even before his death in December 2013. The long-serving president Jacob Zuma resigned under pressure in early 2018 after a slew of corruption scandals. One-quarter of the population is unemployed. Many of the apartheid-era townships remain crowded, rat-infested slums with inadequate resources. The country's old companions—crime and violence—still plague many areas. Children of color still don't receive an adequate education. The list of woes the nation and its new president, Cyril Ramaphosa, face is long and daunting.

Yet I can at last admit that I no longer hate South Africa. Many generations will come and go before the country can overcome its sordid history of colonialism and apartheid—just as the United States is taking many generations to come to terms with its shameful heritage of slavery and segregation. I only hope that as time goes on, my former home will not slide back toward the past, and that its fitful progress will ultimately produce the country that its people deserve, the one for which so much blood was spilled.

After a lifetime spent running away from South Africa, I must also admit that I've only been partially successful in that effort. Fueled by my anger and my inexorable drive, I put oceans between myself and my native country, worked like the devil, became a U.S. citizen, and learned what it's like to live in freedom. Yet I realize now that I never fully left South Africa, because pieces of it came with me and live deep inside me still. Hard as I've tried to wrest myself from its grip, it is and always will be a part of me.

Acknowledgments

HIMMET

Foremost, I thank my lovely wife, Debbie Dajee, for her patience and support. She never complained about my long hours and the urgent phone calls in the middle of the night. I am filled with love and profound appreciation. I couldn't imagine a better partner.

I thank also my amazing daughters Olivia Dajee and Isabelle Dajee for their love and encouragement. They inspire me to be a better man. I did this for them.

My brothers Dhiraj and Naresh, my sisters Padma, Hansa, and Harsheila, my sister-in-law Belle, and my cousin Manu Dala I thank for their love and support.

I am grateful to my former professors Dave Murphy, Eoin O'Brien, Donald Hill, and the late Harold Browne for teaching me to be inquisitive, diligent, and innovative.

My talented UCLA mentor Hillel Laks gave me the opportunity to complete my training and provided me the key to the most exciting career—and used his superb surgical skills to repair my heart. I owe him my deepest gratitude.

Gasant Emeran and the late Polly Slingers, former principals of my old school Trafalgar High, risked much to teach their students to think for themselves.

I thank Dr. William Pick, who assisted me with my research in South Africa; Dr. John Malone, who helped me with my research in Ireland; and Anwar Mall, Clive Kirkwood, Lionel Smith, and Howard Philip, at the University of Cape Town, who helped me access my student records.

I've had the desire to write a book about my life experiences since I was born during a unique time when tumultuous events were unfolding in South Africa and around the world. Thousands of miles away from Cape Town, Patrice was the catalyst who transformed my thoughts into words. She reminded me of an archeologist digging in search of rare bones and artifacts. She had the patience to listen to my agonizing story, and I am sincerely indebted to her.

Finally, I give thanks to all the many patients who put their faith and trust in me.

PATRICE

I give thanks to my darling husband, Robert Weinberger, for his unfailing love, support, and encouragement. He told me to do this. For once, I listened.

Thank you also to my wonderful sons Bret Weinberger and Chris Weinberger for believing in me; Bret, for his help with the painstaking task of transcribing taped interviews and his impressive grasp of history; and Chris, for his superb marketing insight. You make me proud.

My dear friend Debbie Dajee kept the iced tea flowing, ran errands, performed numerous clerical duties, and lavished me with undeserved praise.

Holly Monteith at Cynren Press carefully and respectfully nurtured our project to fruition. It has been a privilege to work with her and her crack team of professionals.

Publicist Gretchen Koss, at Tandem Literary, offered keen instincts and impeccable skills; thank you.

Thank you also to attorney Steven Halper for his generosity and wisdom.

I am grateful to all my family and friends, who cheered me on, and the editors with whom I've worked during my career, particularly Barry Stavro, whose admonishments to pay attention to details are imprinted on my brain.

Finally, I thank the man named Courage himself, Himmet Dajee. His dignity, perseverance, and unvarnished honesty have been inspirational. He endured hour upon hour of my poking into the most personal details of his life, never complained when I asked the same question twenty different ways, and remained steadfastly optimistic when my confidence faltered. My gratitude and admiration for him are beyond measure.